BUSINESS
EXECUTION
FOR RESULTS

A PRACTICAL GUIDE FOR LEADERS
OF SMALL TO MID-SIZED FIRMS

M000086598

STEPHEN LYNCH

Business Execution for RESULTS
A Practical Guide for Leaders of Small to Mid-sized Firms

Copyright © 2013 by Stephen Lynch
All rights reserved
Cover design and illustrations: Bianca Te Rito
Structure and format: Wally Bock
Copy editing: Gabriella Deponte
Text composition: Clark Kenyon

All rights reserved. This book was self-published by the author Stephen Lynch
under Stebian press. No part of this book may be reproduced in any form by
any means without the express permission of the author. This includes reprints,
excerpts, photocopying, recording, or any future means of reproducing text.
If you would like to do any of the above, please seek permission first by
contacting us at info@stebian.com

Published in the United States by STEBIAN.com
eBook ISBN - 9780989064804
Paperback ISBN – 9780989064811

PREFACE

One of the most important things you will ever do is get the right people alongside you to help you build your business. I'm no different.

Like a lot of entrepreneurs, I'm creative, excitable, and enthusiastic. The challenge is to make the most of those talents without causing the disruption and uncertainty usually associated with a constant stream of new and "better" ideas. That's why Stephen Lynch has been the perfect person to have alongside me as we have built RESULTS.com.

He is the most disciplined, structured, and thorough person I've ever worked with, and he reads more and researches more than any person I've ever met. The tools and process that Stephen has shared in this book represent the perfect complement to entrepreneurs or business leaders who want to combine their ideas with an absolutely proven, tested, comprehensive system for bringing their vision to life and keeping it thriving.

Every time I want to change direction or propose a new strategy, I know that my idea will have to pass the Lynch test. Stephen makes sure that what we do conforms to the best research and best practices available. That's a big part of the reason that we have been so successful in staying ahead of the competition and expanding our company around the world.

The tools and process you'll read about in this book have passed the Lynch test. They've also passed the test of the marketplace. They work for RESULTS.com and for our clients around the world. I know they'll work for you, too.

Ben Ridler
CEO, RESULTS.com

STEPHEN LYNCH

What do a police officer, a champion bodybuilder, a pharmaceutical sales and marketing manager, a nightclub DJ, a software entrepreneur, a chief operating officer of a strategy consulting firm, and a business execution expert have in common? The answer: Stephen Lynch, who has been and done all that.

Jim Collins likes to talk about "getting the right people on the bus," but Stephen Lynch could have pulled that bus, and all those people, right down the street. That's the kind of challenge you have to meet when you compete in New Zealand's Strongest Man competition, as Stephen did in 1993.

That same year, he was crowned Mr. New Zealand bodybuilding champion. Five years earlier, Stephen had made winning that national title his primary goal. He studied bodybuilding and nutrition and what top performers actually did. Then he put together a rigorous strategic plan and followed it, winning the title on his first attempt.

That's the model he's used ever since in his personal life and in business: First you set a big goal. Then you gather information to find out what the facts are and what the top performers do. Next, you develop a well-considered strategic plan that you follow every day, pausing at regular intervals to assess the environment, your goal, your progress, and your strategy.

As the Chief Operating Officer of RESULTS.com, he has been responsible for researching and developing the strategic planning and business execution practices that are incorporated into the RESULTS.com software and consulting services.

Stephen has personally consulted with the leadership teams of hundreds of client firms around the world, supporting them to create and execute their strategies using the exact methodology he writes about in this book, *Business Execution for RESULTS*.

Stephen has written articles for *The Economist*. He is a voracious reader of business and personal development literature and maintains contact with the world's leading business thinkers. He and his wife, Bianca Te Rito, enjoy weight training, yoga, and travelling to new places.

What Others Have to Say About Stephen

"Through RESULTS.com's unique methodology, Stephen has helped us set and accomplish a number of important strategic priorities. Stephen is a skilled facilitator who consistently keeps our management team focused on setting and executing against strategic goals. I've seen lots of consultants who help with strategic planning, but very few who add value in driving execution. I appreciate that Stephen has helped enable us to execute on a number of important, measurable, lasting changes in our business."

Dan Clifford
Co-founder, AnswerLab

"We hired Stephen at TaskUs in the beginning of 2012. He worked with my business partner, our team, and me for the entire year. Over the course of the year, we doubled our revenue and grew our team rapidly. The principles that Stephen taught us were directly responsible for much of this success. I highly, highly recommend working with him."

Bryce Maddock
CEO, TaskUs

"We've been working with Stephen (RESULTS.com) for a year now. Through working with Stephen, we have undergone a major transformation in how we run the business. Our clients have even commented on how much more professional and more mature our business looks. It's been one of the best investments we've made in the business. I've noticed that I carry some of the same thought techniques to working on various projects."

Laura Davis
President, Strategic Consulting Solutions

"I cannot speak highly enough of both Stephen and RESULTS.com. They enabled us to think far more clearly about our objectives: how to stay on track, how to hire/fire intelligently, and how to truly take responsibility for our actions. I would HIGHLY recommend Stephen; I truly believe that ALL companies, big and small, will benefit from his expertise."

David Harris
Managing Partner, Teffic

"I highly recommend Stephen and the RESULTS.com process to help grow and improve your business. He has helped us develop our strategy and fine-tune our execution with excellent results! Stephen was very professional and clearly knows how he can best bring value to his clients. The whole process has taken our company to another level!"

Mike Fritz
President, DWFritz Automation

"As a CEO, I often feel like I'm standing on an island. Having Stephen alongside me as an Executive Coach, Accountability Partner, and Advisor has been game changing. The single greatest endorsement I can provide on Stephen's behalf is that, through his coaching, counsel on infrastructure, and operational background, he was able to help me get my company set up in such a way that I was able to vacation with my family overseas for five weeks and never once worry that things weren't being handled by my Senior Leadership Team."

Jonathan Davis
CEO, HireBetter

"When RESULTS.com says they are the 'business execution experts,' they are not exaggerating. Stephen is someone who gets results. He has expert knowledge on strategic planning and execution. He is very organized and dedicated. Working with him took my business to the next level. Before working with Stephen, we did not have clarity on our long-term vision and goals. Stephen helped us to build the strategy from the ground up and to execute on our plan. If you have the opportunity to work with Stephen, I would highly recommend it."

Mike Del Ponte
Founder, Sparkseed

"Stephen's the leader you trust, because he delivers on his promises. I've seen him over the past seven-plus years address and deliver solutions for a multitude of business challenges for clients around the world, and for his own company in serving those clients. His leadership is one that encourages engagement, participation, enthusiasm, passion, and commitment. People like to be held accountable, especially with a leader like Stephen who sets a clear direction, communicates openly and clearly, gives people the tools they need, and helps others help themselves. And in those tough situations that leaders often face, he's a friend who delivers on his promises of integrity, confidentiality, heart, and sage advice."

Zane Safrit
Business Consultant, Radio Show Host

"I have been incredibly impressed with Stephen Lynch. He is a person of extremely high integrity, substantial intellect, and keen strategic insight, all with the ability to communicate and connect superbly with clients. I am a huge fan of the RESULTS.com system and highly recommend Stephen as one of their leading experts."

John Spence
Author of *Awesomely Simple: Essential Business Strategies for Turning Ideas into Action*

Acknowledgements

Thank you to the following individuals for their inspiration, contribution, and support:

Bianca Te Rito

My beautiful and talented wife. Thank you for designing the book cover and all the illustrations. Most of all, thank you for continually asking, "So when are you going to write your book?" and pushing me to get it done. You are the most passionate, hard-working person I know. You inspire me every day. I am grateful for your love and support on this adventure we call life.

Wally Bock

My friend and writing coach. I had plenty of raw content but soon realized that content alone does not make for a great book. I am deeply grateful to Wally for organizing and knocking my content into shape. Wally has an extraordinary wealth of business and publishing expertise to share, and he is a pleasure to work with. I really miss the weekly chats we had when working on the project together. We have become firm friends.

The team at RESULTS.com

Thank you for the inspiring work you do every day that makes a positive difference to the lives of the business leaders we touch. It really is true that a small group of passionate people can change the world if they put their minds to it. A special thank you, Ben Ridler, for your entrepreneurial courage and for sharing my desire to "go big or go home" and make a difference on a global scale. Thank you also to past and present members of our leadership team, whose belief in me has sent me on the adventure of a lifetime to spread the "Results love" around the world: Simon Mundell, Kendall Langston, Lisa Carter, Tony Vine, Rod Hill, Ian Mackenzie, Scott Morris, John Leduc, and Tim O'Connor.

My consulting clients

I have been privileged to experience firsthand hundreds of industries, business models, and company cultures in my strategy consulting work with clients. It has been the greatest learning experience of my life to work alongside you, supporting you and cheering you on from the sidelines on your journeys to success.

Contents

ILLUSTRATIONS

Getting Started

I was standing on stage at the Mr. New Zealand bodybuilding competition. It was the final part of the show. They were handing out the trophies, and it was down to one other contestant and me. I was confident that I had done enough, but, just as in boxing, you can never be completely sure what decision the judges are going to make.

All the years of brutally hard training and the torture of following pre-contest Spartan diets had culminated in this moment. I closed my eyes and waited.

> "and Mr. New Zealand...
> 1993...
> open men's heavyweight division...
> Stephen Lynch!"

I leaped into the air and waved to my mother and sister, who were jumping up and down at the back of the theater.

What joy! What relief! I had achieved my big goal, but it was time to begin something new. I retired from bodybuilding right there and then and set a completely different goal, which has brought me to the point of writing this book. But the way I achieved that goal is similar to the way I've helped companies achieve their goals in my work at RESULTS.com.

My journey to Mr. New Zealand had started eight years before. My uncle was a police inspector in charge of New Zealand's diplomatic protection squad. His stories of life on the job seemed much more exciting and interesting than the dry accounting and statistics I was studying at university.

I decided to join the New Zealand Police. At five feet, nine inches tall, I just made the height requirement, so I decided that a little weight training before I started the police academy would help give me more physical presence and strength to do the job. It did, and it also took me in a direction I never anticipated.

After two years of weight training, I'd gained a lot of muscle and literally re-shaped my physique. I was genetically blessed with a body that responded well to weight training, and I devoured all the books I could find on the subject to further my results.

It was the mid-1980s; Arnold Schwarzenegger had become the world's most recognizable movie star, and his success carried the fringe sport of bodybuilding into the mainstream. I decided that I wanted to look like Arnold and emulate his success. When the gym manager suggested I should enter a novice bodybuilding competition, I jumped at the chance. When I won my first novice competition in 1988, I set the big, big goal of becoming Mr. New Zealand by 1993.

Thousands of people begin weight training every year, and many don't set any goals at all. Others abandon the process without achieving much. Only a tiny percentage of people who begin weight training set significant goals and achieve them. That's about the same as in business.

According to the International Health Club Association, 90% of those who join health and fitness clubs will stop going regularly within the first 90 days. That's similar to the percentage of business strategies that fail. Harvard professor Robert Kaplan says that "various sources have reported failure rates at between 60 and 90 percent." One study by Bain and Company of large companies in eight countries from 1988 through 1998 found that 87.5 percent of the companies failed to achieve the profitable growth that their strategies called for.

Why don't those strategies work? The executives who develop them are smart and savvy. But it's like becoming Mr. New Zealand: Anyone can create a plan that sounds like it will succeed, but to achieve the goal you have to do more, whether you're a business executive plotting strategy or a bodybuilder out to win an important title.

Business Execution for RESULTS starts with great goals. Becoming Mr. New Zealand was the biggest goal I could conceive of at the time. Today, I help organizations set the kind of big goals that make great companies.

Setting a goal feels good, and it's tempting to think that setting the goal is enough. It's not. You have to create a winning strategy to achieve your goal.

It seems like there's a lot of help available. Every year, thousands of books and articles and blog posts promise to reveal the latest, newest, neatest, unheard-of-until-now way to create a great strategy. Most of them get things only partly right.

The truth is that there's no magic way to achieve anything important. I was fortunate that a more experienced bodybuilder took me aside and told me the truth very early in my quest. He showed me that the way to the goal I wanted didn't involve the great new ideas and "revolutionary" products I was reading about in the magazines.

The way to the goal I wanted was following a rigorous, disciplined process from beginning to end. First, I had to do my homework to find out what really worked for my body. Then I had to use what I'd learned to plan a strategy that would take me to my goal. And then I had to follow that strategy every day, even on days when I didn't feel like it or when more pleasant distractions were beckoning me. That same outline holds for creating a business strategy that delivers results.

You start the process by setting what Jerry Porras and Jim Collins call a "Big Hairy Audacious Goal." In this section of the book, I'll show you how to create a goal that will keep you and your team energized and focused.

Once you've set your goal, you need to do some serious homework. In the second section of this book, I'll guide you through a rigorous process to identify important facts about your industry, the market, and the larger environment. That's the section on "Doing the Analysis."

The analysis gives you information to make the wise choices that are the essence of good strategy. That's what we'll cover in the section on "Making Key Decisions."

There's only one more thing: making sure your strategy actually delivers results. That's the equivalent of the training I had to do every day on my way to becoming Mr. New Zealand. There are really two parts to this process:

In the sections on "Getting Ready to Run" and "Success by the Numbers," you'll break your strategy down to the basic action level. I'll share my insights on how to set Key Performance Indicators and build a team of

A-Players. Finally, in "Maintaining Thrust," you'll learn ways to keep going strong, all the way to your goal.

There are no tricks. There is no magic. If you're seeking a simple, easy way to create a strategy that delivers results automatically, you can stop reading right now. You won't find it here.

Business Execution for RESULTS is a process that utilizes best-of-breed concepts and tools. You will find a process that thousands of RESULTS.com client firms have used to drive better business results. I know the process works. And I know it will work for you, but you have to work the process for that to happen.

Now, if you're ready, let's get on with setting a Big Hairy Audacious Goal so you have something inspiring to work toward.

Big Hairy Audacious Goals

MIGUEL "MIKE" SOTO LOVES TO climb mountains. Lots of people climb mountains for the fun of it; they love the outdoors, the exercise, and the challenge. Mike loves those things, too, but he also set a goal of climbing the highest mountain on each continent, and he set that goal right after his first rock climbing experience. Here's what he told a friend a couple of years later:

> I wanted something that would challenge me. If I decided to be a top rock climber, I'd get better and always try to do better than last time, but setting the goal of climbing the highest mountain on every continent gave me a clear goal and forced me to get better faster. It was more fun, too.

Business goals are a lot like mountains: If you want to get to the top, you need to plan and marshal your resources. You need to develop skills and habits, and practice the basics of climbing diligently. The thing that separates great mountain climbers from the rest – and great companies from the merely good – is the mountain they choose to climb.

I love the term "Big Hairy Audacious Goals," coined by Jerry Porras and Jim Collins in their book, *Built to Last*. Porras and Collins abbreviate that to BHAG (pronounced "bee-hag"). They don't ever give us a narrow definition of a BHAG, but they give us many examples. Probably the best known is President John F. Kennedy's "man on the moon" goal.

You have to remember that things didn't look bright for the USA at the time. The Russians seemed to be beating the USA to every space milestone. Americans were worried and not very confident about how they would fare in the "space race." That's why many commentators thought the president was crazy when he suggested this BHAG to a Joint Session of Congress on May 26, 1961:

> I believe that this nation should commit itself to achieving the goal, before this decade is out, of landing a man on the moon and returning him safely to the earth. No single space project in this period will be more impressive to mankind or more important for the long-range exploration of space; and none will be so difficult or expensive to accomplish.

The goal was huge and – even more important – no one, including President Kennedy, had any idea of all the things that had to be done for the country to reach it. I think of setting a BHAG as being like throwing your hat over a huge wall and then figuring out how you're going to get it back. So you begin this process by throwing your hat over the wall and thinking, "I want my hat back. Now I need to figure out how to get over this wall and get it."

Big Hairy Audacious Goals have four characteristics:

- They're very, very, very big.
- They will take several years to achieve.
- You won't yet know the details of how to accomplish the goal when you set it.
- The goal is specific enough that everyone will know if you achieve it.

In 2002, Walmart was the biggest company in the world, and that astonished a lot of the business press. *Fortune* magazine asked the question: "How did a peddler of cheap shirts and fishing rods become the mightiest corporation in America?" Part of the answer lay in setting a BHAG.

Long before he founded Walmart, Sam Walton was setting Big Hairy Audacious Goals. He started doing it with his first store. Right after World War II, Walton combined his savings with a loan from his father and bought a Ben Franklin dime store franchise for a store in Newport, Arkansas.

That's where he sat down and wrote out his BHAG: "Make my little Newport store the best, most profitable variety store in Arkansas within five years." Then he figured out how to do it.

He kept the store open longer than other stores. He bargained hard with suppliers but also placed larger orders than other variety stores did, so suppliers had an incentive to deal with him. Then he passed the savings on to his customers in the form of lower prices. By 1948, his store had tripled in volume and was not only the most profitable store in Arkansas but also the most profitable in a six-state region.

Sam Walton kept on setting Big Hairy Audacious Goals, and Walmart kept finding ways to achieve them. In 1977, he set the goal of more than doubling sales to $1 billion by 1981. The company passed that milestone in 1979. In 1990 – when he set a revenue growth target of $125 billion by 2000 – Walmart's revenue was about $30 billion, and it was already the largest retailer on the planet. The company achieved its goal one year ahead of schedule.

Let me make three important points:

First, a BHAG doesn't have to be about growth. Walt Disney used BHAGs related to products. In 1934, he set the goal of creating the first animated feature-length film. Industry pundits called it "Disney's Folly." After all, they said, animation might be fine for short films, but no one will sit in a theater and watch over an hour of animation. When *Snow White and the Seven Dwarfs* was released in 1938, people flocked to the movie houses. The film earned more than 100 times what it cost to make.

Second, BHAGs are audacious, which means they're risky. Boeing had great success with its BHAGs of building the 707 and 747 aircraft. With the 747, though, that success came only after slow sales for the airplane nearly killed the company. And their BHAGs to build other airplanes have not worked out as well.

And third, there's always a risk when you set a BHAG, but you can improve your odds of success with a disciplined process of goal setting and execution, like the process you'll learn in this book. BHAGs are perfect for amazing and successful companies that want to make a giant leap in performance, companies like AnswerLab.

AnswerLab is a flourishing company in the growing field of user experience research (UX). Co-founder Dan Clifford says that AnswerLab helps clients understand how their digital products (websites, mobile apps, etc.) are perceived by their users. Then the clients can "improve areas that are confusing or frustrating so that they can deliver compelling products that are easy to use."

AnswerLab is up against some Goliath competition in firms like Nielsen and Forrester, but it is carving out its own niche in the research industry and positioning itself as a leader. It has been profitable, increasing revenue in every year since its founding in 2004. And it's on the *Inc.* 500 list of the fastest growing privately held companies. In other words, AnswerLab was a successful firm before it started using the process that you will learn here.

The people at AnswerLab have grown the company mostly by doing some simple but often difficult things. They're obsessed with being responsive to customers and turning decisions around quickly. They make sure to bring up issues that their clients might not think of, which adds value, prevents surprises, and builds trust.

They work hard at recruiting A-Players, too. While other firms may rely on interviews when hiring, AnswerLab assigns candidates an analytical exercise as homework and then spends time discussing it with them.

AnswerLab made several wise choices in its first years. Many companies go after venture funding and then find themselves captive to investor expectations. AnswerLab chose to stay private and fund growth from profits, adding office space and staff as needed and not "just in case."

Another wise choice involved marketing strategy. Many start-ups go after small clients first, planning to move up to larger clients later. But Answer-Lab went after the big fish right from the beginning. That means a longer start-up cycle, but it also means that the clients you get are credibility builders. Their first client was Honda, and the list now includes Amazon, PayPal, ESPN, Genentech, Wells Fargo, and Walmart.

I didn't need statistics to tell me that this was a successful company. When I visited their San Francisco office to begin working with them as a client, the atmosphere was electric. I knew right away that I was with intelligent, energetic people, experts in user experience research who were committed to delivering great results.

AnswerLab was like many companies I've worked with. They're made up of ambitious learners, and they know many of the concepts that have been covered in business books for years. Successful companies are doing a lot of things right, but often they don't have the kind of focus and alignment necessary for dramatic improvement. That's where Business Execution for RESULTS comes in.

Before I begin the strategic planning process with any company, I ask key people to fill out questionnaires about their Core Values, Core Purpose, and goals. The results at AnswerLab were the same as for many other companies – you ask ten people the same question, and you get ten different answers!

AnswerLab was a successful company, but the owners wanted to take it to the next level and dominate their niche. To make that happen, they needed everyone to understand their Core Values, Core Purpose, and goals in the same way and to then adopt a disciplined strategic planning and execution methodology to make sure they executed on those goals. That's where the methodology contained in this book comes in.

Let's take a look at the first step: setting a Big Hairy Audacious Goal. According to Jim Collins, that involves answering three important questions in no particular order:

- What can you be the best in the world at?
- What are you passionate about?
- What will drive your economic engine?

Whilst these are good questions, in my experience they do not go far enough in terms of helping you refine your answers. I have taken this framework as a start point and modified it with my additional questions below to make it more practical for the business leaders I work with:

What can you be the best in the world at? Now, that's the best in your world, however you define your world. Your world might be your suburb, it might be your town, it might be your state, it might be your country, it might be the whole world, or it might be the whole universe. It might be your industry or a small part of your industry.

For AnswerLab, their world is user experience research, where they're world-class experts. What can you be best in the world at?

In what category can your company be perceived as a leader or as being meaningfully different from your competitors? This concept is often represented with your Strategic Positioning statement, which we will cover later in the chapter of the same name.

What are you passionate about? Passion defines your Core Purpose, which we'll refine later. Passion is what drives great companies, because people want to work for something beyond the numbers.

So what is it that really gets you out of bed in the morning, beyond earning a paycheck, beyond making money, beyond showing profits? What is the difference you want to make in the lives of your customers?

AnswerLab is obviously passionate about user experience research, but they're also passionate about their relationships with clients and improving the digital world. What are you passionate about?

What drives your economic engine? What is your business model going to be? How will you make money? Where will you get your revenue and profits from in the future?

AnswerLab already had their basic business model in place, so they developed their BHAG around the number of large clients, defined by revenue billed per annum. What drives your economic engine?

You can find more information on creating business models and on understanding how your business makes money in the book *Business Model Generation* by Osterwalder and Pigneur. They do a great job of helping you visualize how your business works.

Look at the diagram on the next page, which I modified from the one in Jim Collins's book, *Good to Great*. Your BHAG is the place in the diagram where the three circles intersect. It's made up of the few things that you can be great at, that you are passionate about, and that you can make money from.

Here are a few more questions to ask yourself that will help you refine your BHAG. This is where I want you to throw your hat way, way over the wall. Think five or ten years into the future and ask how your company will look when you achieve your BHAG.

- What will your operations look like? That might be the number of stores, or it might be the number of factories, the number of customers, the number of just about anything that you can think of.
- What products or services will you offer? They may be something completely different than what you are offering now, or they may be the same. Think about the mix, too.
- What geographic locations will you serve? Don't worry about how to reach them now; we'll figure out how later.

Figure 1: How to find your BHAG

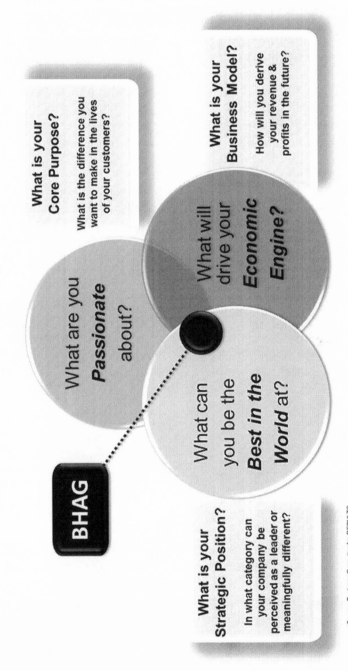

What is your
Core Purpose?

What is the difference you
want to make in the lives
of your customers?

What is your
Business Model?

How will you derive
your revenue &
profits in the future?

What will
drive your
*Economic
Engine?*

What are you
Passionate
about?

What can
you be the
*Best in the
World* at?

BHAG

What is your
Strategic Position?

In what category can
your company be
perceived as a leader or
meaningfully different?

Source: Business Execution for RESULTS

- What's it going to be like to work for your company in the future? Describe what it will be like when you come to work.
- How will you measure success? Revenue and profits are important, but so are other measures. Perhaps you'll win some awards or some form of recognition. How will you measure your success along the way?

There's one more thing: Some people describe a goal as "a dream with a deadline." BHAGs have the emotional power of a dream, but that defini tion is incomplete. To be a good business goal, it needs to be a dream with a deadline and numbers. Here's what AnswerLab came up with back in 2010:

> Be the most trusted brand for user experience research in the world, achieving $500K in annual revenue from each of 20 clients by the year 2015.

What's your BHAG? Remember, it should be exciting, but it should be a little scary, too.

If you are thinking to yourself, "Yes, well, if we do that, and we do that, and if we keep growing at X percent per annum, and keep putting one foot in front of the other, we'll reach this point by year 2020," that's not a BHAG. A BHAG is not a linear path. A BHAG is something you should stare at and think, "How the heck are we going to do that?" You don't know how yet, but you like the sound of it, and you're going to figure out how.

Here's the thing: When President Kennedy set the "man on the moon" goal, no one knew how the USA was going to achieve it. Sam Walton set a goal for his very first store and then figured out how to achieve it. That's what Disney did with animated features, too. The whole idea of a BHAG is that it's an exciting goal that inspires you to figure out how to achieve it.

What's Your BHAG?

By now you have probably come up with a long list of things that describe what you want your business to become at some point far into the future, and that's great. Some companies create walls full of words or collages full of pictures to describe their ideal future, and that's a great exercise, too, but now I want to force you to crystallize your dream into a clear, concise statement using what I call my "Twitter Rule"; that is, if you can't communicate a concept within the length of a Twitter post, then it is too long.

See if you can state your BHAG in a short, concise statement of 140 characters or less.

When you're ready, turn the page and learn about Core Purpose and Core Values.

Core Purpose and Core Values

LET'S TALK ABOUT REAL LIFE for a minute. Think back to Sam Walton, sitting there in his first, very small store in Newport, Arkansas. He didn't start by drafting a statement of values or defining his purpose. He wrote out a Big Hairy Audacious Goal, and, as he worked out ways to achieve it, he also developed the values and purpose that still drive Walmart today.

While he was working to achieve his BHAG, he discovered that bargaining hard with suppliers was a good thing, but only if he became important to them. He learned that the best formula for him was to pass the savings along to his customers. Those were the beginnings of the Core Values and Core Purpose for every store he ran after that. As his career evolved and he started and grew Walmart, those concepts would change in detail, but not at the core.

Decades later, long after Walton's death, efficient procurement is a Core Value at world-beating Walmart. Hard bargaining is part of that, but so are efficient logistics and information systems. The idea of savings evolved into "everyday low prices" and a Core Purpose: "To give ordinary folk the chance to buy the same things as rich people."

Your Core Purpose and Core Values are important, but I have found that spending too much time on them too early in the process can lead to inefficiency and frustration. I'll introduce you to the key principles of Core Purpose and Core Values in this chapter. Then you can have them in mind while you work on some key strategic decisions. That way you'll be prepared, when we revisit the principles later in the book, to define your Core Values and Core Purpose and use them as a guide for improving your results.

Core Purpose

Remember that, if you're going to climb that big BHAG mountain, you need to give your people a compelling reason why they should climb mountains with you at all – that's your Core Purpose. There are positive and negative human reasons why having a purpose is important.

Money is important, but it's not enough. People want to work for something beyond the numbers. Purpose adds energy and emotion. The classic example is the story about the two bricklayers toiling away on a job. A passer-by asked each one what he was doing.

The first bricklayer replied, "I'm laying bricks, of course." And he went back to his work.

But the second bricklayer's eyes lit up as he told the questioner, "I'm helping to build a great cathedral!"

When people have a purpose that goes beyond the numbers, they pour more energy into their work. They give it more thought. They're more likely to be what the management gurus call "fully engaged."

But when numbers are all there is, it's more likely that people will have a short-term focus. Dr. Richard Hagberg, an organizational psychologist who has studied corporate purpose, says that companies who are fixated on hitting quarterly and even daily targets often don't produce sustainable profit growth.

It's different when companies have a Core Purpose. Dr. Hagberg found that a combination of challenging goals and a clearly articulated purpose characterized the companies that delivered the highest returns.

When all you've got is numbers, you get bricklayers who do their job for a paycheck and nothing more. But when you've got a well-understood Core Purpose, you get engaged people pouring their energy and ideas into building your version of a great cathedral.

That's a good thing. Research by Gallup indicates that companies in the top quartile for engagement are more productive and more profitable than companies with a less engaged workforce. The employee research firm ISR studied more than 500,000 workers' engagement and concluded that a highly engaged workforce drove both productivity and profits. Hewitt Associates tracked 300 companies over five years and found that increases in employee engagement preceded improvements in financial performance.

After we've worked through the strategic planning process and you've made some key strategy decisions, I'll ask you some questions. Your answers will help you define your Core Purpose. Read them over now so that your mind will pick up clues to your answers while you work on your strategy:

- Why does your company exist, beyond making a profit?
- What are you really passionate about?
- What difference do you make in the lives of your customers?
- Your product or service will evolve over time. What do you do for your customers that transcends whatever your current product or service offering is?

Core Values

There are several complicated academic definitions of "values," but I prefer something simple. Your values are the behaviors you expect from your people. Values are clear statements of how you expect people in your company to act.

There are no studies I'm aware of about the profit-building power of values per se, but there are plenty of studies about the power of culture. Culture is the collection of internalized rules of behavior for the people in your company. Those rules form the basis for your Core Values. By identifying your Core Values and making them explicit, you shape your culture. That's important, because your Core Values and culture do several things for your company:

- Your Core Values provide a moral compass for your people. They can help your staff decide on the right course of action, regardless of the challenge they face.
- Your Core Values establish a basis for consistent decision making by everyone. When people share the same Core Values, they tend to make decisions using the same principles.
- Your Core Values give you some guides for hiring, rewarding, disciplining, and firing. Think about companies with strong Core Values and cultures like Nordstrom, Southwest Airlines, Zappos, or Enterprise Rent-a-Car. People often say that "a certain kind of person" does well there. Those are the people whose personal values match the company's Core Values.

Here's the catch – simply writing down some rules and turning them into a statement of Core Values doesn't work. Your Core Values must be unique to your company and reflect the values you have. An excellent example of what that looks like is a value statement by the New Zealand firm James Wren & Co. It's simple and to the point:

Three coats means three coats.

James Wren & Co. has been a high-quality painting contractor in the city of Dunedin for over a century. It's a business where firms come and go and where many compete on price. Wren is different. Managing Director Richard Daniell explains the ideas behind their unique Core Value statement this way:

> It is easy in this industry to get away with one less coat if you tint your sealer/primer coat, and many of our opposition are known for it. We know you can do it, too, but you end up with inferior finish, so we choose not to take the shortcut approach, often to the detriment of securing a contract. It is core because we are prepared to miss out financially by not securing contracts; it is spoken virtually every day by either one of our shareholders, estimating staff, tradesmen, supervisors, or clients. Examples of it are given in every edition of our newsletter. We incorporate this Core Value in nearly every decision we make.

That's a lot of words, but Wren gets all of that into a single sentence: "Three coats means three coats."

That simple value statement reminds their people not to cut corners when preparing a bid. It tells buyers such as architects and interior designers why Wren's bid may be higher than the competition's. And it reminds their workers on the job about what really matters.

Imagine you're fifteen years old, and you've just left school and joined this painting firm as your first job. When Core Values are expressed like this, you know exactly what sort of behavior is expected of you. It's not an ambiguous and generic word like "integrity." It is a clear statement of "Here's how we do things around here."

Keep that in mind as you work through your basic strategic choices. If you've been in business for a while, you've probably already developed some of those unwritten rules – "the way we do things around here" – that you'll sharpen into your Core Values later. In the meantime, here are some questions I want you to answer and think about:

- Who in your company is a living example of "the right behavioral standards"?
- What is your company known for?
- What behaviors are so important that you'll fire anyone who doesn't consistently demonstrate them?

Think about your Core Purpose and Core Values as you work through the analysis and strategic planning in the next few chapters. You'll get to answer the questions and sharpen your Core Values and Core Purpose so they can help drive results in the section called "Getting the Most from Human Capital."

To create a winning strategy, Business Execution for RESULTS begins with rigorous, disciplined analysis. Turn the page to get started on the road to better results.

Doing the Analysis

By 1962, Sam Walton had come a long way from that little store in New-port, Arkansas. He had dime stores scattered across Arkansas, Missouri, and Kansas. He was the largest independent variety-store operator in the country, thanks to his strategy of driving hard bargains with suppliers for ever-larger orders and passing the savings along to his customers.

The popular image of Sam Walton is of a folksy old billionaire who drove a pickup with his dog in the back. He was folksy, all right, and he drove a pickup that often had one of his dogs in the back. But he also had an economics degree from the University of Missouri, and he was obsessive about doing his homework.

He knew that doing the hard work of gathering information and analyzing it are the first steps toward making the wise choices at the core of an effective strategy. He gathered information in every way he could think of.

Walton read the trade magazines. He talked to his suppliers' salespeople when they called on him. He got out of the office to visit his stores, the competition, and his suppliers. As he travelled and read, Walton sucked up information and ideas. He knew every one of his competitors from reading about them in business magazines, from meeting them at trade conventions, and from visiting their stores. By the late 1950s, Sam Walton was a master retailer, and he knew exactly how his stores compared with every competitor's stores.

You need that kind of knowledge to make wise strategic choices. In the next chapter, you will do your own detailed competitive analysis, using the Five Forces framework developed by Michael Porter.

Sam Walton didn't just analyze the competition. He paid attention to the ways the country and society were changing.

By 1960, Americans owned 74 million automobiles, more than double the number in 1940. Fifteen percent of households in the USA had more than one car, more than double the percentage of just a decade earlier.

Those cars and improved roads made families more mobile. In more rural areas, towns were becoming closer than ever in terms of travel time. Walton saw that his stores could count on an ever-larger trading radius, drawing customers from what used to be great distances.

Walton's analysis of his industry and of society helped him spot the opportunity that would lead him to create Walmart. He knew that the dime stores, like the ones he owned, faced a threat from a new kind of store. Not only that, there was one he could observe up close.

In 1958, Texas retailer Herbert Gibson began converting his Gibson Products wholesale operations into retail outlets. One of them was in Fayetteville, Arkansas, and Gibson's new "discount" store was taking business away from one of Walton's dime stores. Walton looked at what Gibson was doing, what was happening in other parts of the country, and what he knew about how the USA was changing. In 1962, he opened the first Walmart in Rogers, Arkansas.

That year marked a watershed in general merchandise retailing. In addition to the first Walmart, the first Target store opened in Roseville, Minnesota, and the first Kmart opened in Garden City, Michigan. Discounting was a good idea, but it didn't work for everyone.

Gibson's stores are now gone. Woolco, Ayr-Way, GEM, and Fisher's Big Wheel have come and gone. Target has been successful, and Kmart has had its ups and downs. In the meantime, Walmart became one of the largest companies on earth. One reason for Walmart's success is that Sam Walton did the research and analysis that helped him make good strategic decisions.

Strategy is choosing the right actions to ensure success today and tomorrow. And the only way you can be sure you're choosing the right actions is to do some serious analysis.

You'll begin with industry analysis, using a framework for analyzing your industry by answering some important questions. You'll have to dig up the information you need and wrestle with your answers to the questions. When you're finished, you will have a clear picture of the competitive environment where you do business.

That's important, but you need more if you're going to make wise strategic choices. That's the time to take a step back and analyze the major trends in society that affect your marketplace. I use the acronym PEST for Political, Economic, Sociological, and Technological trends.

Then we'll zoom way in for one more area of important analysis. In the chapter on "Market Analysis," you'll answer questions that tell you about your customers and what they think of you and your products and services.

Sam Walton did that kind of analysis, too. From talking to his customers, he found out that they used coupons and shopped at special sales, but what they really wanted was what he came to call "everyday low prices." That became a core part of Walmart's strategy, and it probably wouldn't have happened without that analysis.

Analysis is important work, and – I warn you – it won't be easy. It will be like my bodybuilding workouts. Some days, everything will go perfectly, and other days will be really, really hard. But if you want to create a winning strategy that delivers results, you've got to have the discipline to dig deep and do the analysis. It's that simple.

Business Execution for RESULTS works. Thousands of RESULTS.com clients all around the world have used this process to create something more than a strategic plan – they've used it to create a winning strategy that drives results.

But the process will only work for you if you work the process. That's easy when the process is fun. Clients get excited when they set a Big Hairy Audacious Goal. They love the planning process. But most of them don't love the grind of doing the industry analysis, the part you're about to do.

Just about every company does some kind of strategic planning. Many of them do it at a "strategic planning retreat." That's why every consulting firm that helps with strategic planning gets calls every week asking if it can come out and facilitate a strategic planning retreat or planning session.

When someone calls RESULTS.com out of the blue asking if I can facilitate their strategic planning retreat in a couple of weeks, I usually surprise them by saying, "No!" Then I qualify that by saying: "Yes, I can help, but you need to do some serious homework first, and it is probably going to take you at least a month. When you've done that, I'll talk with you about meeting to facilitate your planning process."

The reason is simple: If you want to create a strategic plan that will set you up for future success in your industry, you have to do the analysis first. That takes time.

Each of the analysis exercises you're going to work through will take you at least a week, and probably more. The whole analysis process may take you more than a month; it needs to be rigorous and thorough, or it won't equip you to create a winning strategy that produces results.

Here's how to do your analysis well: Select the team that will do your strategic planning. You don't want any more than ten to twelve people in the room at any one time. So pick a core group of six to eight members. They should attend every meeting. You can supplement them at individual meetings with subject matter experts or stakeholders.

Each member of the core team should answer all the questions himself or herself. Some questions may require research. I know that you'll talk to each other about the process, but it's important that members of the team answer the questions in their own ways.

Team members should send their answers to someone who will put them together so that everyone can see all the responses to each question. Then have a meeting where you work out the answers to the questions, but this time as a group.

Professional basketball coach Pat Riley used to say, "No rebounds, no rings," to remind his players that if they wanted the success represented by a championship ring, they had to do the hard work of rebounding, playing defense, and practicing. I turn that into "No analysis, no results."

If you're ready for the hard work of analysis, it's time to turn the page and tackle "Industry Analysis."

Industry Analysis

WHAT IF YOU WERE AN army general with a battle to win? What would you want to know?

You'd probably want a map. A map tells military strategists what the territory is like, where the ground is high and low, and where there are rivers and roads.

But maps do more than portray the terrain. If you're a general, you want to know where the enemy troops are. You want to know how many of them there are and what kind of firepower they can muster. You'll also want to identify other variables that could influence the battle, so you can think about how to deal with them.

In this chapter, I'm going to help you draw your map and populate it with information. I'm going to give you a framework for analysis and then take you through a disciplined process to make sure that you wind up with an accurate map, one that you can use to plan your actions.

This won't be easy. This chapter is the big one, the hard one, the long one, the tough one. It's going to be mentally taxing and intellectually draining, but when we're through you will be ahead of most companies in the world.

Most firms don't do this kind of analysis at all. They think that they "know" all about their industry. The fact is that they probably don't. Researchers at the London Business School established that many businesspeople don't know the basic facts about their industry, even though they're quite sure they do.

Warning: Do not take things for granted. Check and verify.

Many companies that do some industry analysis don't do it in a rigorous, disciplined way. They spend a day at an offsite and pull something together. Or they hire a consultant to write a report, but they never discuss it.

Keep that in mind as you work your way through this chapter. It will be hard work. But when you're done, you'll have the information you need to create a winning strategy that will set you up for future success in your industry.

Business Execution for RESULTS requires that you leave no stone un-turned. Sometimes when you turn over a stone, a nasty threat slithers out. You need to be aware of that and make sure you're taking the right actions to deal with that threat. Alternatively, sometimes when you turn over a stone, you may find a jewel of an opportunity. What could you do to take advantage of that opportunity?

There's one more thing about process that's important: There's often a bet-ter answer than the first one you come up with. If I'm in the room with you, I can push you to get a better answer. For now, you'll have to do that part of the hard work yourself. So, if you're ready, let's begin working on your strategy with a bit of history.

People have done business since the beginning of recorded time. In fact, many of the old clay tablets that archeologists have unearthed have con-tained business records. But while people have done business for thou-sands of years, they've only done strategy the way we will for about fifty of them.

Successful businesses have always had a clear idea of what they wanted to accomplish, and they often did some planning. But before July 1, 1963, they didn't do strategy the way we think of it today. On that day, Bruce Henderson opened the doors to his own consulting operation, which would become the Boston Consulting Group.

Henderson is the father of modern corporate strategy. He added two things to the way businesses before him had looked at the business landscape. Henderson introduced the idea of competition and the concept that a com-pany's strategy should be the result of a rigorous and disciplined process. Almost every firm that helps companies develop strategy uses ideas and tools derived from what Henderson developed.

The other giant of corporate strategy is Michael Porter. Porter's huge con-tribution was to create a framework for analyzing industries and competi-tion that helps companies like yours ask the right questions to develop a winning strategy.

Consulting firms around the world adopted Porter's methods. In her book, *I'm Sorry I Broke Your Company*, Karen Phelan describes how Porter's work was required reading for consultants at Deloitte, Haskins, and Sells and at other firms. But those firms often make two fundamental errors when they apply Porter's ideas:

First, they assume that, when you come up with a sustainable competitive advantage, it is somehow sustainable forever. Nothing lasts forever. You need to thoroughly analyze your situation every year. You must keep innovating and evolving in order to maintain a strategic advantage in your industry.

Second, many consulting firms act as if understanding the marketplace is enough for success. But just because you know something does not mean you do it well. Even good strategic decisions can result in failure with poor business execution and mediocre management. Consider this first analysis as the start of a recurring cycle of analysis and execution. The idea is to use the analysis to gain knowledge and then turn that knowledge into action.

I like Porter's framework because it's a straightforward way of analyzing the competitive landscape of your industry. He defines an industry as "a group of firms producing products that are a close substitute for each other." So think of your industry in that broader sense. It's not only the companies that sell what you sell; it's also the companies that sell products or services that can easily substitute for what you sell. Include the key players in your value chain – from suppliers all the way through to customers.

I confess that when I studied this at university, it all seemed very abstract and theoretical to me. It wasn't until I got out into the business world and began using the framework that I discovered how powerful it is. The framework becomes the way for you to describe your industry and the possible changes in it. It helps you decide what to do. Take a look at the diagram on the next page.

You'll see "Rivalry among Existing Competitors" in the middle. Around the outside there are four dynamic forces that interact with each other through the Rivalry among Existing Competitors. The forces are the "Threat of New Entrants," the "Bargaining Power of Buyers," the "Threat of Substitute Products or Services," and the "Bargaining Power of Suppliers." We're going to analyze all those forces in detail.

Figure 2: Michael Porter's Five Competitive Forces that shape industries

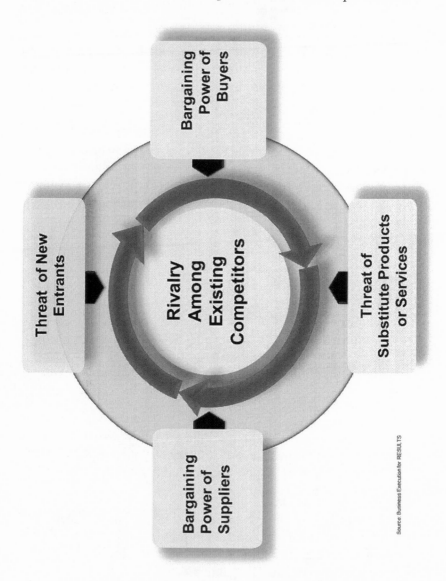

Source: Business Execution for RESULTS

When you're done with the Industry Analysis, you will have a map of the industry and a sense of the forces at work in it. Then you can begin to plot your strategy using that map.

Now, let's review each of the forces in detail. For each one, I'll offer you some general thoughts. Then there will be a series of questions that you need to answer. Don't rush through this. You'll get more value if you analyze one force at a time before moving on to the next.

I will ask you questions about your industry as it exists right now. I will also ask you to forecast what your answers might be to these same questions three to five years into the future. Some people challenge me by saying that it is impossible to predict what will happen that far out and that planning that far into the future is a waste of time.

I always smile and share this quote from Jeff Bezos of Amazon.com, who as you know, competes at the forefront of the rapidly changing tech industry:

> If everything you do needs to work on a three-year time horizon, then you're competing against a lot of people, but if you're willing to invest on a seven-year time horizon, you're now competing against a fraction of those people, because very few companies are willing to do that. We can't realize our potential as people or as companies unless we plan for the long term.

With that story, companies quickly realize that planning at least three to five years out is probably a good idea after all. Besides, I'm going to introduce you to a process in this book that frees you from dependence on long-term forecasts by using a cycle of analysis, execution, and review to create great results.

When I'm working with a client, I give them these questions as a series of pre-work exercises. They go away and obtain the answers. Then I challenge their thinking and conclusions well before we get together for an actual strategic planning and decision-making session.

So let's get right to it. Here is the first of Michael Porter's Five Forces:

Rivalry Among Existing Competitors

Increased global competition and commoditization are driving down prices in many industries. If you've got many competitors and they're offering
similar products and services, you don't have much power. If your customers or your suppliers can't get a good deal from you, they'll go somewhere
else. You must be meaningfully different from your competition if you
want to have power in your industry.

There's no right or wrong answer to any of the questions, but you may find
that different team members have different ideas. That's good, because it
should spark conversation. To get the most benefit from that, I suggest that
you do what I do when I work with companies:

Give everyone on your team the questions and have them come up with
their own answers, without talking to each other. This is best done as a
take-home exercise. Then come together and work out the group's answers.

Here are your questions. The first ones are about the state of your industry.

- Where is your industry today in terms of the industry life-cycle
  stage? Is it in the introduction phase? Is it in the growth phase?
  Is it a mature industry, or is your industry going into decline?
- Before you go on, think about the future. Where will your industry be in terms of the life cycle within three to five years?
- What is your industry growth rate today? What will it be within
  three to five years?
- What's the average net profit for firms in your industry? How do
  you think that will look within three to five years?

The answers you came up with about industry life cycle and growth rate
will help you get an idea of the general trends in your industry. The next set
of questions is about competition of all kinds and will give you an idea of
who your competitors are and where you may have advantages.

- How many competitors are in your industry? How many will
  there be within three to five years? Will the industry consist of
  a lot of small players, or is it going to consolidate and be domi-
  nated by a few large companies? Will there be more or fewer
  competitors within three to five years?

- Who are the major players now, and who do you believe will go on to become the major players within three to five years? You may want to make some notes about why you've made those judgments; they'll come in handy when you compare your list with the ones created by other team members.
- What is your current market share versus your competitors? What do you expect it to be within three to five years?
- How much money do you really need to win in this industry? How much capital do you need right now and within the next three to five years?
- Globalization is significantly affecting many industries now. What impact do global competitors have on your industry? How will that change within the next three to five years? What companies and countries are we talking about? Why will they affect your market?
- What about this concept of commoditization? In an industry that's become commoditized, all the product and service offerings are perceived as essentially the same. When that happens, price is the only way to distinguish among competitors.

Right now, you probably think you're different, but are you really?

- How differentiated are you from your competitors?
- More important, what do your customers think? If you haven't done so recently, you may want to talk to a few customers before you answer this question.

Another way to come at this is to answer these questions:

- How price competitive is your industry?
- Will this change within three to five years? Why?
- Who in your industry has cost advantages?
- Who will have cost advantages within the next three to five years?

Let me give you some thought starters. Consider the following:

- Who in your industry has economies of scale?
- Who has a leaner cost structure?
- Which competitors are outsourcing? Companies often do that to reduce costs.

Now review those same questions, but while looking out three to five years.

Next, analyze sustainable competitive advantages. Start with your own company:

- Do you have a sustainable competitive advantage, something that cannot be copied easily?
- What about the firms you compete with?
- Now, look three to five years out. What do you see then?

Here's something I want you to look at closely:

- Are any of your advantages really sustainable? Is anything a sustainable advantage that is based on intellectual property where underlying patents may be expiring? Be honest. How hard would it really be for a competitor to replicate what you do?
- Which competitors are likely to engage in "spoiler tactics" like predatory pricing, price wars, or product dumping? This typically occurs in a mature industry, when some large players are desperately trying to hang on to the status quo. They may bring in teams of lawyers to prevent new entrants and substitute players from getting off the ground. How do you see it now and within three to five years?

Now, step back for a moment and consider:

- What key moves do you think your competitors are likely to make in the near future? What about within the next three to five years?

Here's the big question:

- Based on what you've uncovered in Rivalry among Existing Competitors, what Strategic Moves do you need to make to address the issues you have identified, now and within the next three to five years?

Highlight your answers to this last question so you can revisit them later.

Threat of New Entrants

New entrants can easily weaken your position if it doesn't cost much in terms of time, money, or skill to enter the industry. It's easier for newcomers to enter if there are no incumbents with economies of scale. It's easier if there's little or no protection for key technologies or if new entrants can bring significant cost advantages to the market. On the other hand, if barriers to entry are high, your competitive position is somewhat protected.

- Are there any industry barriers to prevent new entrants from coming into your industry right now? What about within the next three to five years?
- What are the capital requirements that new companies must come up with in order to enter your industry? How much money do they need to get started and get underway? What about within the next three to five years; how do you see that changing?
- Are there any new, potentially disruptive competitors sneaking in under the radar? Are they offering what the incumbent firms might currently consider to be "inferior" products? Are they starting to gain traction by serving the low-cost, low-profit part of the industry?
- This is the classic "Innovator's Dilemma," a term coined by Professor Clayton Christensen who says, "An innovation that is disruptive allows a whole new population of consumers access to a product or service that was historically only accessible to consumers with a lot of money or a lot of skill." This type of disruption typically occurs when the incumbent competitors offer products that are vastly superior in terms of performance or functionality. The new entrant offers a much lower-spec product at a dramatically reduced cost and starts gaining market share at the low end of the market. The incumbent competitors typically ridicule the new entrant's offerings as being of lower quality. However, over time the new entrant evolves its product, and, before you know it, it has driven a wedge underneath you. Some examples of this are how the traditional print media viewed blogs, how the full-service airlines viewed "peanut-serving" Southwest Airlines, how Microsoft Office viewed Google Apps, and how American automakers viewed Japanese (and more recently Korean) cars.

- What about learning requirements? Are some special skills, qualifications, licenses, or experience required to actually get into your industry? What are they now, and how do you see that changing within the next three to five years? Will those changes make it harder or easier for new firms to enter your industry?
- Are supplies important? Think of supplies in the broad sense. "Supplies" could mean raw materials. They could also mean people with particular talents, or they could mean access to office space or production capacity. What does that look like now? What will it look like within the next three to five years?
- Do new entrants need access to distribution channels? Think about a distribution channel as everything necessary to get the product in front of a customer. What does that look like now? What about within the next three to five years?
- How loyal are your customers to existing firms? How loyal are your customers to you and your current competitors? Are your customers just as likely to switch and go with a new entrant to your industry? What does that look like within the next three to five years?
- Is it hard or easy, expensive or inexpensive, for customers to shift to new entrants? Are there any sticky factors that make it inconvenient for customers to switch? Are there any lock-ins or anything that you can do to enhance loyalty and customer longevity? What about within the next three to five years?

I've already touched on globalization. Let's revisit it in the context of possible new entrants into your industry:

- What is the threat of new entrants coming in from other geographic locations? What does that look like within the next three to five years?

When new firms attempt to enter your industry, chances are the existing firms aren't going to sit still and simply let them come in.

- When a new entrant appears, what sort of retaliation can they expect from existing firms? How is that likely to play out within the next three to five years?

Before we move on, there's one more question:

- Based on what you've uncovered in Threat of New Entrants, what Strategic Moves do you need to make to address the issues you have identified, now and within the next three to five years?

Highlight your answers to this last question so you can revisit them later.

Threat of Substitutes

Your power is affected by the ability of your customers to find a different way of achieving a similar solution or outcome to your product or service. Very often, new technology opens new possibilities that can result in competition. The compact disc replaced vinyl records, then online downloads and streaming replaced CDs. In each case, the technology provided a different way of delivering the same product: recorded music. That's one kind of substitution. The objective is to listen to music, and the different technologies offer substitute ways to accomplish that.

There's another type of substitution that's often harder to spot. It's the product or service that's not in your industry but that helps a customer achieve the same goal as your product. If you're in the lawn mower business, you obviously compete with all the other lawn mower companies. Customers can substitute a competitor's lawn mower for your lawn mower.

But you also compete with anything that eliminates the need to purchase a lawn mower. So you compete with a lawn service that will mow the lawn, and you also compete with a low-maintenance yard design that doesn't require mowing at all! Keep both types of substitution in mind as you go through the questions on the Threat of Substitutes.

- What technology changes are on the near horizon, right now, that might impact your business model? What new technologies have been developed in the last few years? How might they affect your business model within the next three to five years?
- What about structural changes in the way your industry operates that could also impact your business model? Is there anything going on right now? What about within the next three to five years?
- What substitutes are available today? Make a list. How will that change within three to five years?

- How does each substitute perform compared to what you're offering?
- How do customers perceive the difference between your product or service and any substitutes?
- How willing are your customers to seek out alternative solutions or different ways of achieving the end result that you deliver?
- How costly or difficult is it for customers to substitute one offering for another?

Look at these last five questions and consider: What will change within the next three to five years?

Finally, based on your analysis of the Threat of Substitution,

- What Strategic Moves do you need to make to address the issues you have identified, now and within the next three to five years?

Highlight your answers to this last question so you can revisit them later.

Bargaining Power of Suppliers

How much power do your suppliers have to dictate prices to you? That power is determined by how many suppliers there are, their size and strength, how unique they are, and how easy or costly it is for you to switch to another supplier. The fewer supplier choices you have and the more you need their help, the more powerful they are. And, in some industries, your suppliers or your supplies could be the skilled labor you need.

- Let's start with a list of your major suppliers: How will it change within the next three to five years? Why will it change?
- What about the cost of supplies? What's the cost now? What do you see the cost being within the next three to five years, and why?
- How much negotiating power do you have with your suppliers? How do you see that playing out within the next three to five years? Why?
- Do you have access to alternative sources of supplies? Are you able to shop around? What does that look like now? What do you see it looking like within the next three to five years, and why?
- How costly is it in both time and effort for you to switch suppliers? How is that likely to play out within the next three to five years?

Forward integration is when a firm moves down the value chain and begins to compete with firms it supplies. Manufacturers begin selling to retailers, for example, or wholesalers open their own retail outlets. Or perhaps your highly skilled staff quit to set up their own firm in competition with you.

- What is the threat of forward integration in your industry, where the suppliers actually decide to get into your game? And what does that look like within the next three to five years?

Now take a moment to review your answers in this area.

- What moves are your suppliers likely to make? What moves are they likely to make in the near term, but also within the next three to five years? And what are the reasons for this?

Finally, based on your analysis of the Bargaining Power of Suppliers,

- What Strategic Moves do you need to make to address the issues you have identified, now and within the next three to five years?

Highlight your answers to this last question so you can revisit them later.

Bargaining Power of Customers

Are there customers like Walmart in your industry? If there are, then you understand the bargaining power of customers. Walmart requires suppliers to meet detailed specifications for every product. Those specifications can include the packaging, labeling, and shipping details.

In general, the more important any individual customer is to your business, the more bargaining power that customer has and the less you have. For your industry, the bargaining power of customers is determined by the number of vendors they have to choose from, how meaningfully different they perceive you to be, and the cost to them of switching from your products or services to those of your competitors. Your customers also wield power to the extent that they can influence other customers to buy from you or not.

Let's do some disciplined analysis of how things are in your business.

- Start by making a list of your major customers. How will that list be different within three to five years? Why?
- How much power do your customers have to set prices or dictate terms to you? What does that look like now? What is it going to look like within the next three to five years, and why?

Here's a tricky one: How much can your customers influence others to buy from you or not? A few years ago, this was not a major concern in most industries. Then came the web and social media. Individual customers can now sing your praises or tell their tales of woe to millions. Here's one example of how powerful that can be:

In 2008, musician Dave Carroll took a trip via United Airlines from his home in Halifax, Nova Scotia, to Omaha, Nebraska. While sitting in the airplane on a stop at O'Hare airport in Chicago, Carroll and others saw baggage handlers throwing bags, including his guitar, on the tarmac. Sure enough, when Carroll got to Omaha, he discovered that the neck of his $3,500 guitar had been broken.

He approached United workers in Omaha, but no one wanted to help. When he got back home and filed a claim, the airline denied it, saying he hadn't filed it within 24 hours. After trying several different ways to get satisfaction, Carroll wrote a song. He titled it "United Breaks Guitars" and put it up on YouTube.

The video was viewed several million times in the first month after it was posted. The mainstream media picked up the story. People cancelled reservations. The company's stock price dropped. One pundit claimed that the incident cost United enough to replace Carroll's guitar 51,000 times.

Granted that "United Breaks Guitars" is a particularly creative complaint about a very poorly handled incident, it still illustrates how customers now have a way to share their pleasure or displeasure about your products and services. If you're in an industry where customers post ratings and comments about you and your competitors, you're most at risk.

- So what is your customer's ability to influence other buyers, and how do you see that playing out within the next three to five years?
- What is the customer's perception of differentiation between

you and your competitors? You might think you're different, but what does the customer think? And how different are you really? Be specific. What is that customer perception? How do you know? How will that change within three to five years?

- How costly or easy is it for customers to switch to one of your competitors? How sticky are you? What sort of lock-in do you have? What sort of loyalty do you enjoy? Will that change within the next three to five years?

Backward integration happens when a firm moves up the value chain and begins to compete with firms that they bought from before. Retailers may establish their own distribution centers instead of using wholesalers. Your customers may develop their own offerings to replace yours, or they may decide to do it themselves rather than purchase from you.

- What is the threat of backward integration in your industry? How will that change within the next three to five years?
- Now put yourself in your customers' shoes. What moves could they make within the next three to five years? How would that affect you?

Based on what you've uncovered in Bargaining Power of Customers,

What Strategic Moves do you need to make to address the issues you have identified, now and within the next three to five years?

Highlight your answers to this last question so you can revisit them later.

Whew! That was a lot of work – a good, hard analysis workout. But you're not done with analysis just because you've gathered data, information, and perceptions about your industry. What's going on in the world outside your industry that will affect your strategy? That's what we'll analyze in the next chapter.

Environmental Scanning

PEST Analysis

You've done a lot of important analysis already. You've used Michael Porter's Five Forces to gather information and impressions about your industry. Business Execution for RESULTS requires that you now zoom farther out and consider how changes in the world around you will affect your industry and your strategy.

We're going to do some environmental scanning using a simple model described by the acronym PEST. PEST stands for the Political, Economic, Social, and Technological forces in the business environment. Those forces act on your industry from the outside, as shown in the diagram on the next page.

Remember Sam Walton: In 1960, when he analyzed the general merchandise retail industry, he noted that people like Herbert Gibson were moving into discount retailing. He experienced that as a threat within his industry.

But he also looked outside his industry and analyzed what was going on in the country, and that analysis supported the idea of discount retailing. Americans were riding the post-World War II economic surge. The Baby Boom was adding to the number of potential customers. The government was building roads, including the Interstate Highway System, to connect cities and towns. And Americans were driving more and more cars.

Political, economic, social, and technological changes all made it possible to draw more customers from a wider area to large discount stores. These were the outside forces working on the retail industry, and they made discount retailing a great strategy.

We're going to analyze each of the PEST factors. As you do the analysis, I want you to make notes about how the PEST forces will affect your industry and what actions you'll need to take in the coming years. Let's begin with a look at political forces.

*Figure 3: PEST Analysis – macro forces that impact the business
environment*

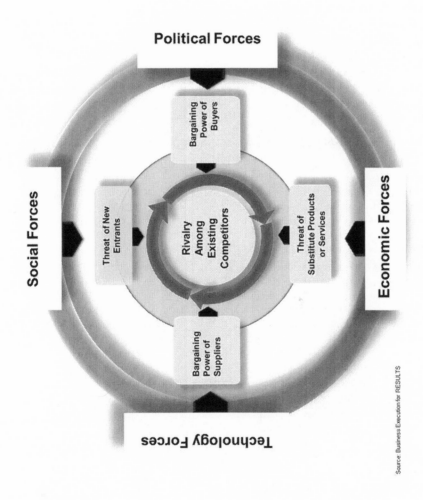

Political Forces

What are some of the political factors that could potentially impact your industry? Here's a list of possibilities; you can come up with others. Remember that if you do business in more than one jurisdiction, you should analyze the political forces in each one.

- Which political party is in power?
- How stable is the political situation where you do business?
- What specific laws and regulations govern your business?
- Make a list of the important political and regulatory factors. How do they affect you now? How will that change within the next three to five years?
- What Strategic Moves do you need to make as a result of any political threats or opportunities that you see, both now and within the next three to five years?

Highlight your answers to this last question so you can revisit them later.

Economic Forces

What are the economic factors that could influence your industry? Here are some factors:

- Economic growth
- Interest rates
- Exchange rates
- Inflation
- Availability of credit

You should be able to identify other factors. If you do business in more than one country, you're likely to have different economic factors and answers for each one.

- How attractive is your industry to outside investors in venture capital or private equity? How about conglomerates looking for acquisitions?

Think about all these forces and how they affect your industry today and also how things may change within three to five years.

- What Strategic Moves do you need to make as a result of any economic threats or opportunities that you see, both now and within the next three to five years?

Highlight your answers to this last question so you can revisit them later.

Social Forces

Social factors are changes in the way people live and act. They include changes in demographics and in the number and distribution of people, and also sociological factors like values and habits.

- What social factors could influence your industry?

Among demographic trends, it may be the aging of the population in your area or the age distribution of the workforce itself. Think about the attitudes of the people that you employ and those who are your customers. Perhaps there are health or environmental issues that specifically affect your industry.

- How about the way people communicate now and are likely to communicate in the future? How could that impact your industry? Think about the online behaviors of people, whether your own staff or your customers.
- And what about society's changing beliefs, attitudes, and values? How do you see those impacting your industry?
- What Strategic Moves do you need to make as a result of any social threats or opportunities that you see, both now and within the next three to five years?

Highlight your answers to this last question so you can revisit them later.

Technological Forces

Technology is one area of life where we see changes almost daily. That's an exaggeration, of course, but even if you're young you can trace significant changes in technology that have happened in your lifetime. Look at their influence and think about other changes in your industry that will be driven by technology.

- Think about new technologies that will specifically touch your industry. What new technologies are affecting you right now? What about those that you think are likely to make a mark within the next three to five years?
- What is the rate of technology adoption or obsolescence in your industry? How quick are people to embrace new technologies?
- The mobile Internet and social media are changing the way we do business today. What do you think that's going to be like within the next three to five years?
- What are the hot new technologies in your industry right now? How will they change the industry within three to five years?
- Who are the technology leaders in your industry? What are they doing today that you may be doing within three to five years?
- Are there any technologies out there that could completely disrupt your current business model?
- What Strategic Moves do you need to make as a result of any technological threats or opportunities that you see, both now and within the next three to five years?

Highlight your answers to this last question so you can revisit them later.

OK, you can take a breath now. You've had another good workout with the environmental scanning. There's only one big chunk of analysis left. Let's zoom in to analyze your target market customer, the one right at the center of your bull's-eye.

Target Market Analysis

I'D COMPLETED THE REFRESHER ON firearms safety, and now I was on the firing line with a pistol in my hand. I've served in the Territorial Army (New Zealand's equivalent of the USA's National Guard) and on the NZ police force, so I've done my share of rifle and pistol shooting. But it's not a hobby or even a significant interest, so it had been almost 20 years since I last used a firearm.

We were there because my wife, Bianca, wanted to know what it actually felt like to fire a pistol. That may sound odd to an American, but, in New Zealand, where we both come from, guns are strictly controlled, and they are only available to the police, armed forces, and members of pistol shooting clubs. It is rare for a member of the public to have even seen a gun, let alone fired one.

I booked a half-day introductory training session with a tutor at the LAX firing range in Los Angeles. We'd completed our lesson, and now the range master was giving final instructions before we were allowed to fire the Glock pistols. "Remember," he said, "you have to aim for the bull's-eye if you want to hit the target. If you just aim for the target, you will be more likely to miss it."

That's as true for marketing as it is for pistol shooting. Business Execution for RESULTS demands that you aim for the center of the target if you want to hit the target consistently. That sounds logical, but it's not an insight that comes naturally to business leaders.

I've encountered several companies that seemed to think that it was best not to aim at all. A plumbing company might describe its customers as "anyone who needs plumbing services." A toy store could say its customers are "people who buy toys," while a toy manufacturer would describe its clients as "companies that sell toys."

It sounds reasonable, but actually it is a huge mistake. It's like aiming in the general direction of the target: You're not likely to hit something that matters to you, and you waste a lot of ammunition.

Those companies saw things differently after we worked through the exercises in this chapter. And when I ask companies who've gone through the process what was most helpful to them, the most common answer is "getting very clear on who our target customer is." It's a huge "Aha!" moment for them. You can take their word for it, or you can take the advice of experts like Dr. Philip Kotler.

He is the S.C. Johnson & Son Distinguished Professor of International Marketing at the Kellogg School of Management and the author of the most widely used marketing textbook. He has this to say:

> There is only one winning strategy. You need to carefully define the target market and then direct a superior offering to that target market.

That's good advice. If you pick a target and shoot at it, you're more likely to hit something important, something profitable for you. But that's when the advice from my shooting instructor kicks in: If you really want to be successful, you need to shoot at the bull's-eye in the center of that target.

Right now you may be thinking, "But if I aim at one type of customer, won't I miss some of the people who would make really good customers?" The answer to that is, "Yes, but."

It's almost a paradox, but if you do a good job of target marketing – aiming at the center of the target – you're likely to attract more good customers, not less. That's the research-supported advice of Doug Hall.

You may know Doug as one of the panelists on the *American Inventor* television series. Or you may have read one of his books, like *Jump Start Your Business Brain*. Doug is the CEO of Eureka! Ranch, a company that helps clients deliver "meaningfully unique" products and services to their target markets.

I've had the pleasure of spending time with Doug. He says many wise things, but here's the important one to guide your marketing:

> Delight the few to attract the many.

Let me clear up a few points. Your target market is the center of your marketing bull's-eye. They're the people or companies you have in mind when you create and develop your product or service and when you create your marketing communications.

They may not even be the customers that you sell the most to. But by tailoring your offerings and your marketing to that bull's-eye group, you will also attract many other customers who sit in the outer rings of the target. "Delight the few to attract the many."

If someone who's not in your target market begs to buy your product and offers you money, of course you'll sell to them. You just won't spend precious time, money, and effort trying to attract them.

Here's an example of how this works. I learned about this one from Marcus Buckingham. The company is called Tesco.

Tesco is a UK-based retailer, and it happens to be the third largest retailer in the world. An important component of its business is Tesco supermarkets. When I'm working with a client group I often ask them, "Who are Tesco's target customers?" The answer I usually get is, "Anyone who buys groceries." That's the wrong answer.

If you walk into a Tesco and want to buy food, Tesco will certainly sell it to you. They'd be fools not to. But you're not their target customer. You're not at the center of the bull's-eye. The center of Tesco's bull's-eye is "the harried housewife."

Because they know that the center of their bull's-eye is that harried housewife, Tesco can arrange everything so that they become her favorite place to shop. It starts with location.

Tesco locates stores in places that are easy to get to and in areas where there are a lot of housewives. They design their stores for the harried housewife's convenience. That means wide aisles, since the housewife will probably be shopping with children. They stock the items she wants to buy and sometimes stock related items together so shopping is more convenient for her. When the harried housewife gets to the checkout, she wants a speedy, child-friendly checkout.

What Tesco has defined is the person who is at the center of their bull's-eye. They know that if they delight the harried housewife they will create a solid, sizeable, and loyal customer base. But they know something else, too. They know that other people will be attracted by the wide aisles, convenient shelving, and fast checkout.

Let's take a look at this from the other side. Seth Godin says that "a product for everybody is a product for nobody." He says that your offering should stand out like "a purple cow." If you delight your customer, he or she will come back and give you the most powerful marketing force in the world: great word of mouth.

You can probably understand this from your own life. Let's say you go to a restaurant and you get a decent meal. You have no complaints – the food was tasty, the atmosphere was pleasant, the portions were good-sized, and the price was fair. You're satisfied. But you won't go out and tell your friends about it. You won't say, "Hey, I just had a satisfactory dining experience." It wasn't remarkable.

But what if you and your spouse went to that same restaurant and you had an absolutely delicious Italian meal? The restaurant looked like an old-time Italian restaurant, with red wine already on the table and a menu on the wall. While you're eating, an accordion player named Gordy stops by and asks for requests. You ask for "Fly Me to the Moon" by Frank Sinatra, because it reminds you of when you got married, and Gordy plays a spirited rendition.

Would you tell your friends about that restaurant? I bet you would, like I just did. That restaurant is in Las Vegas, and it's called Battista's Hole in the Wall. Here's an important point: You may not like Battista's. You may not like Italian food, or you may not think the food at Battista's is good. You might hate having a musician disturb your dining. That's all OK; it proves that you're not at the center of the target for Battista's. They may not please you, but Battista's delights people who return whenever they're in town and, because it's distinctive, they tell others. Battista's delights the few and attracts many more.

Now, keep that in mind, and let's get back to the disciplined and rigorous process of finding out who's at the center of your bull's-eye. This is the last big chunk of analysis that I'm asking you to do before you move on to making some key decisions.

Handle this block of analysis just like the industry and PEST analysis that you've already completed. Give the process at least a week. Answer the questions individually. Then put all your answers together and come together as a group to work out your group analysis.

We'll start by examining your best customers today.

- Begin by listing your most profitable customers. Describe them. What do they have in common?
- Who are your most influential customers? They're the ones who are most likely to convince or persuade other customers to buy from you. Describe them and identify the commonalities.
- What type of customer has the most potential for growth in the future? Why?

There are some customers who are on all three lists. They're probably the ones who sit at the center of your bull's-eye. Others are on two lists. Think of them as the next ring out from the center. And then there are the customers who are on only one list. They're in the second ring out from the center.

Now we're going to dig a little deeper and come up with some more specifics. The next set of questions is for you if you sell to other businesses. If that's not you, then skip down to the section for a business that sells directly to consumers.

- What industry are your ideal company customers in?
- Where are they located?
- How big are they, in terms of annual revenue or the number of employees?

Be very precise here. You want to tailor your marketing and sales processes to your ideal customer, and different-sized companies handle purchasing very differently.

Now let's look at people as customers. If you're a B2B company, you must do this part, too, because in every company there's a person – a buyer – who makes the decisions. If you sell to consumers, answer the questions for your customers. If you sell to businesses, answer the questions for the buyers you deal with at your client companies.

Figure 4: Who is your target market customer?

Source: Business Execution for RESULTS

- Are your ideal customers male or female? How old are they? This is important because men and women think differently and respond to different marketing approaches. People think differently at different ages, and they have different historical reference points, too.
- Now try to describe their lives in as much detail as you can. Where do they live and with whom? Where do they work? At what sort of job? What's their income? What do they do for fun? What's a typical workday like? A weekend? A vacation?
- Now for some psychographics: What do they value? What do they believe in? What brands do they own or aspire to own? Who are their heroes and role models?
- Now go a little further: What media do they consume? What media do they participate in, such as social media or games?

Analyze the product adoption lifecycle. Where do your best customers fall on the curve? Take a look at the diagram on the following page.

This curve is usually called the Technology Adoption Lifecycle Curve, but it applies in many non-technology industries as well. Some customers like to buy things at the bleeding edge of new technology innovations, soon after they've been introduced. Others prefer to wait until the product goes mainstream. Still others don't buy until everyone else is already moving on to the next big thing. Where do your target customers sit?

- Are they Innovators?
- Are they Early Adopters?
- Are they Early Majority?
- Are they Late Majority?
- Or are they Laggards?

There's no "right" answer. What you're after is the best description of your customers, because each section of the curve corresponds to a different marketing approach. You'll get the most from this exercise if you narrow your selection down to only one choice.

At this point, you should be clear about who you think your center-of-the-bull's-eye target customer is. Now describe the buying process for this customer:

Figure 5: The technology adoption life cycle

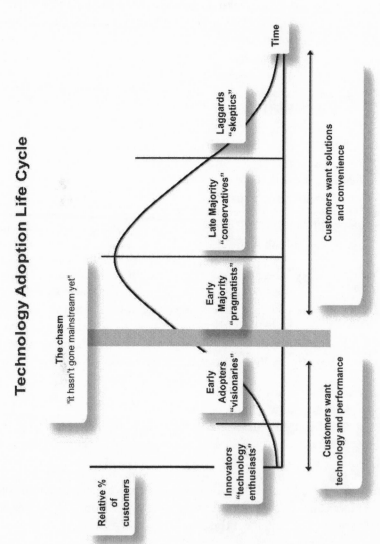

- How do they become aware of your product?
- What process do they go through to make a purchase decision? Describe what happens at each of the stages they go through.
- And what do they buy? What do your ideal customers usually purchase from you? What's the typical value of that purchase, and how often do they buy from you?

If we know those things, we can calculate the average lifetime value of an ideal customer. How much is it? Based on the average lifetime value of each customer to you, how much are you willing to spend to acquire one?

Now it's time to look in the mirror.

- What do those customers think of your industry? What do they like? What do they dislike?

This can be uncomfortable but extremely valuable. In 1988, California voters passed Proposition 103. The measure cut auto insurance rates in the state by 20 percent immediately, along with mandated refunds and other measures.

Proposition 103 was a straightforward message that California voters didn't like auto insurance companies. One company, Progressive, used the proposition as a spur to make changes in the way they handled claims and the way they dealt with policy holders. Before Proposition 103, Progressive was number 13 among auto insurers in the state. By 2002, because of the changes they made, the company was number four in the market.

It wouldn't have happened without Proposition 103. Progressive's president, Peter Lewis, actually called Proposition 103 "the best thing that ever happened to this company."

So make the effort to get the answers as accurate as possible. What do your customers like and dislike about your industry?

Don't stop there. Now comes a really uncomfortable part:

- What do your customers like and dislike about you? How do they think of you? What is their biggest frustration with your company?

I want you to stay inside your customer's head for the next set of questions.

- What is it that they are trying to achieve when they buy from you? What is the job that they want to get done? What is the biggest problem they want solved?

This is a big one:

- What is their greatest desire at the end of the day, and how does your offering make them feel?

Now I'd like you to describe your ideal target customer as a person. There are two ways that this works: Both ways include giving the ideal customer a name and then describing the customer as if he or she were a real, flesh-and-blood person.

The first way is to list the characteristics of the person. The following example is from a company I worked with called The Tile Warehouse in New Zealand. They named their ideal client "Rachel Browne" and describe her this way:

> She is 35-45 years old.
> She is a very hard-working woman.
> She is married to a hard-working man, and they own their own business.
> They have school-age children, and the hubby is on the school board of trustees.
> She attends her children's school camps.
> She drives an SUV, so there's room for everything, including the dog.
> She enjoys a nice bottle of wine with friends, and her friends are just like her.
> She plays tennis, and her husband is into water sports.
> When they are building or renovating, they use the services of interior designers to make sure it is all done properly and it looks good when friends come around!

The Tile Warehouse also did something that might work for you. They created a collage on the wall of their office that represents their target market customer. In this case, they adorned one of their walls with a large composite picture of a person who represented "Rachel" and surrounded her with pictures of brands and images that tell the story of her lifestyle: the car she drives, the house she lives in, the clothing she wears, the jewelry she owns, the brands she prefers, etc.

The benefit of this is that they can look at this collage every day and ask themselves, "What would Rachel think of this?" whenever they are designing a new product or service offering, or crafting their marketing communications.

Here's an example of another way to do the description. It's in a narrative form. The example is for a law firm. Their ideal client is a couple they've named Carlton and Pat Talbert.

> Carlton Talbert is in his mid-forties and a day shift warehouse supervisor at a local supply company. He started with the company over 25 years ago, working on the dock. Since then, he's driven local delivery trucks and worked as a supervisor on the night shift.
> Carlton finished high school here in town where he grew up. He never really had an interest in college, but he's taken a couple of courses at the local community college over the years to learn something he thought was important.
> For fun, he plays poker one night a week and gets together with some male friends to watch games during football season. Other than that, he likes to watch TV in the evening and work around the house on weekends.
> He'll tell you that his wife, Pat, is one reason he's been at the company so long. They've been married 23 years, and she refused to marry him until he'd worked there for, as he puts it, "two long years" and got at least one promotion. Everyone but Pat calls him "Carl." She calls him "C."
> They got married in a local Baptist church, and they're still members there, even though they don't attend every Sunday. Pat does go to an evening Bible study and loves the potluck suppers where she can see what other folks are cooking.

That's just the beginning of a description of the family that runs to about two pages, but it gives you an idea of what they developed. There's no right way to do this, but the more you can turn your analysis into an ideal client who's a real person, the easier it becomes to tailor your offerings and communications and make them as effective as possible. Take the time to develop the most specific and realistic profile that you can.

Now sit back and think about what you've clarified about your target customer. Go back over your notes. When you think you've got a clear idea of who your target customer is, you're ready for the next exercise.

We are going to use my Twitter Rule again: Describe your ideal target market customer in 140 characters or less.

Describe him or her in as much detail as you can, but, because space is limited, you have to choose the most important things to highlight. It doesn't need to be a grammatically correct English sentence; you can string together some key words and phrases, if you like.

Got that? Now, here's another tweet I want you to create: I would like you to describe what it is that your target customer really wants, in 140 characters or less.

Check that your two tweets line up with your detailed descriptions. You have now clearly and concisely stated who your ideal target customer is and what your target customer really wants.

There's one more cluster of things to think about before you leave the area of target market analysis. What you'll read next is based in large part on the work of Gary Hamel and C. K. Prahalad in their book, *Competing for the Future*.

Now that you have concisely stated who your ideal target customer is and what your customer really needs and wants:

- What key benefits do you currently offer to meet his or her needs? What new benefits will you need to offer within the next three to five years? Why?
- Think about the way you interact with your customer. How will that need to change within the next three to five years?
- What geographic areas do you plan to serve, and how will you access those locations?
- What core competencies will you need in order to serve your customer effectively in the future? What type of people do you need?

What training do you need? What technology will you need to meet your target customer's needs? How will that change within the next three to five years?

Highlight your answers to these questions so you can revisit them later in the chapter on Key Strategic Moves.

Congratulations! If you've answered all the questions I've asked and come up with individual and group answers, you're already far ahead of most companies, including your competition. That's because everybody talks about industry and customer analysis, but very, very few firms take the time and make the effort to do this kind of rigorous and disciplined analysis. We'll start putting some of that analysis to work in just a bit, but right now, I want you to turn the page and let's make sure we've dotted the i's and crossed the t's.

Before You Go On

When I work directly with a client, I'm right there to make sure they do things to a proper standard. When you don't have someone like me around, I know it's easy to gloss over some parts of the work, especially in the analysis you've just finished.

Business Execution for RESULTS requires that you make sure you've done everything right before moving on to the more fun parts of the process. I want you to review the questions in the book and your answers and analysis.

Have you answered every question thoroughly and completely? Do the research necessary and come up with the answers before you go on.

Have you worked out all your answers as a group? If not, do that before you move ahead.

As you worked your way through the analysis, I asked you to make several notes about actions you need to take within the next three to five years and to highlight them. Now I want you to pull all those proposed Strategic Moves together and put them on a master list that you'll use when we begin decision making.

When you're satisfied that you've done everything completely and well, please turn the page.

MAKING KEY DECISIONS

Introduction

In 1988, I was in the same position in my quest for Mr. New Zealand as you are right now in your quest for great business results. I had set my BHAG, and you have, too. I had done research and analysis to learn the key factors I needed to take into account in order to achieve my goal, and you have, too. Now it's time for some key decisions.

Goal setting alone is not enough. You need to choose a wise strategy in order to achieve your goal. Strategy is making smart choices about what actions you will take to get the results you want in the future. That's what this section is all about.

All my choices had to support my big goal of winning the Mr. New Zealand title, so let me share something with you that very few people know. There are lots of people with great-looking bodies in the gym or on the beach, showing off their muscles. They may consider themselves to be bodybuilders, but they're not the ones who win the big competitions. The champion bodybuilders are covered up for most of the year.

My research told me that I needed to do some very specific things. One was that I had to forego looking good in the short term in order to build the kind of body that would be able to win the national title later. I needed to bulk up, increasing my body weight by 50 percent (I actually grew from 190 pounds to 280 pounds, at a height of 5'9"). If you saw me at the gym or on the beach in those bulking years, I wasn't showing off my body at all. I was the one who stayed covered because of the way I looked.

Bulking up meant forcing myself to eat huge amounts of food whether I felt hungry or not – for three years! In a normal day, I ate two whole chickens, a large steak, plus several eggs, several slices of bread, rice, oatmeal, protein shakes, and more. Bulking up also meant ferocious workouts that literally made me vomit or faint.

On the plus side, I got bigger and bigger. On the minus side, the process gave me a huge body with a head that looked like a pumpkin. The heavy weight training ensured I never got fat, as most of the calories I was consuming were converted into muscle, but "bloated" is probably the word that comes closest to describing the way I looked. Trust me, I was the last one to be showing a lot of skin at the beach! I looked more like something out of professional wrestling. Little kids would stop me in the street and ask, "Are you a wrestler?"

And then, when it came time to think about competing in the Mr. New Zealand contest, I had to turn everything in reverse. I had to follow an extreme deprivation diet to strip away all traces of body fat and reveal the new muscle I had built underneath. In the months before the national final competition, I went on a near-starvation diet, counting every calorie to get to the weight, the body fat percentage, and the "cellophane-wrapped muscle" look that would win the title. I think that was the hardest part of all, but it was among the wise choices I had to make about training, diet, and preparation if I wanted to become Mr. New Zealand.

You need to make wise choices for your business, too, and some of them won't be glamorous at all. In fact, sometimes they'll be just the opposite of what every other company and the pundits think is the best strategy.

Remember AnswerLab? The conventional wisdom was that they should acquire venture funding so they could grow rapidly; AnswerLab chose to use the founders' resources and its profits to fund growth. Most tech service firms go after small clients first to build their reputation and then move up to larger clients; AnswerLab went after big clients from the beginning.

Those strategies didn't look "right" at the beginning. But they were right for AnswerLab's goal, company, and industry. They were wise choices.

Sam Walton made wise choices, too. When Walton started Walmart in 1962, he made some smart decisions that are still part of Walmart's strategy 50 years later. Walton decided to place large orders with selected suppliers and pass the savings along to Walmart customers. He decided that he would make a low-price strategy work by being ruthlessly efficient and working with suppliers to keep getting better. Just about every other general merchandise store had sales events and used special coupons to boost sales. Walton decided to forego those in favor of "everyday low prices."

Most of Walton's competition probably thought he was crazy. But those Walmart strategies were right for the company, Walmart's customers, Walmart's goals, and the competitive environment.

That's what you'll do in this section. You'll make some wise (but not necessarily easy or popular) choices so that you have a strategy that's right for your goal, your customers, your company, and your competitive environment.

First, you'll decide on your **Value Discipline**. A value discipline identifies the basic things you must do to distinguish your company if you're to have any chance of attaining a position of leadership in your industry. I'll give you three basic value disciplines to choose from. When we work with clients, this is the place where voices start to get raised and chairs get thrown. Making wise decisions is hard, but it's the key to creating a winning strategy that you can execute for RESULTS.

You need to identify your **Core Activities.** You'll identify things you should keep doing, things you should stop doing, and things you should start doing.

Once you know what your Value Discipline will be and you've clarified your Core Activities, you'll start the process of deciding how you'll craft the messages that tell your target market customers why they should buy from you. I've devoted four chapters to that process: "Meaningful Marketing," "Strategic Positioning," "Key Benefits," and "Brand Promise."

When you're ready, let's get to work. Turn the page to find out more about Value Disciplines.

Value Disciplines

In 1957, Jim Brown had an important decision to make. The man who ESPN has called the greatest all-around athlete ever was finishing an impressive college sports career. Brown had earned a varsity letter in four sports at Syracuse University. He won All-American honors in two of them. And he had offers to play both baseball and football professionally.

Jim Brown had to choose a game. So do you. The name of the game is: Value Discipline.

In Business Execution for RESULTS, a Value Discipline is the way that you deliver value to your customer. It's also the skeleton of your strategy. You'll choose a Value Discipline based on who your ideal target customer is and what your ideal target customer values most. So think about your ideal target customer for a moment, the one who's right in the center of your bull's-eye. What's most important for those customers?

Is low cost the most important thing for them? Low cost can be low price, but sometimes it's lowest overall cost of ownership. Sometimes it's lowest cost of time and irritation, because they want a supplier who is efficient or consistent and dependable.

Does your ideal target customer demand the very newest and best? Is that what's most important?

Perhaps your ideal target customer thinks that a personalized solution or customized product is most important?

Take a moment to analyze your ideal customer. Which of these three things do they value most? Remember that every customer would like every benefit, but one value is most important. Got it? Let's see how Value Disciplines match up with customer preferences.

Value Disciplines were first described in a *Harvard Business Review* article and then in the book *The Discipline of Market Leaders* by Michael Treacy and Fred Wiersema. Their basic premises are simple:

> Different customers buy different kinds of value. You can't hope to be the best in all dimensions, so choose your customers and narrow your value focus.

And

> Producing an unmatched level of a particular value requires a superior operating model – a machine – dedicated to just that kind of value.

You've analyzed your target customers, and you've tentatively decided what kind of value matters most to them. Here's an overview of the Value Disciplines to help you finalize your decision.

Operational Excellence

Operational Excellence is the Value Discipline you'll choose if your ideal target customer values low cost more than anything. If you're going to deliver low cost in any form, you must be ruthlessly efficient. Everything you do needs to serve that goal while you constantly streamline your process and drive out waste and cost.

Walmart and Southwest Airlines are two of the best-known companies that have chosen Operational Excellence as a Value Discipline. For more than half a century, Walmart has constantly improved purchasing and logistics to assure that the lowest priced goods come in the door while they also fanatically improve internal operating efficiency.

This Value Discipline isn't just for huge companies. One of my clients, Los Angeles-based Pearl Paradise, is an online retailer out to dominate the global market for pearl jewelry by offering prices that are as much as 80 percent below bricks-and-mortar retailers. In their own words, they want to offer "the best price-for-quality ratio in the industry." That means sharp buying and hyper-efficient operations, true Operational Excellence.

Product Leadership

Product Leadership is the Value Discipline for you if your ideal target customer wants to have the newest and best above all else. You need creativity and the ability to commercialize ideas quickly. Everything you do should serve the goal of providing your customers with the latest and greatest. You'll concentrate on innovation, product development, and market exploitation.

Apple in the Steve Jobs era is the best-known example of a Product

Leadership company. On October 23, 2001, the company introduced the iPod line of MP3 players. In subsequent years, the iPhone and iPad have followed. Each of those products established a standard that everyone else aimed for.

Procter and Gamble (P&G) is another company that's chosen Product Leadership. The company holds more than 30,000 patents and 60,000 trademarks. They even have a position for innovators called Master Marketing Inventor. Doug Hall held that title at P&G before he left to start his Eureka! Ranch.

The P&G lesson is that you can't rest on your laurels. Around the beginning of this century, P&G evaluated its new product development and decided that it could do much better. The company had become very much a closed shop and only looked inside itself for new ideas. In fact, the joke was that the phrase "not invented here" was invented at P&G.

The company responded by developing a program to bring in more ideas from outside and partner more with other companies. They called the program Connect and Develop (C+D). The idea is to connect with other companies and develop new products. At the same time, P&G worked to integrate their innovation process into the cadence of their business.

Customer Intimacy

Customer Intimacy is the Value Discipline for you if your ideal target customer wants a personalized solution or customized product more than anything. Companies that choose Customer Intimacy usually offer a wide range of choices and concentrate on providing each customer with a specific solution to their problem. Treacy and Wiersema say that Customer Intimate companies "don't pursue transactions; they cultivate relationships."

You're probably familiar with many of the top firms that select this discipline. They're the ones that the business magazines and speakers tell those great customer service stories about. Think Nordstrom or Zappos or Ritz Carlton: Those companies have developed strong cultures that empower frontline employees to make decisions that will delight the customer. I think Amazon is another Customer Intimacy example.

Amazon offers a huge range of products. They started with books, of course, but you can now purchase a wide selection of appliances, sports gear, computer equipment, music, movies, and even grocery items on Amazon. The company has developed technology to help you make better buying decisions.

The technology is called "collaborative filtering." It's the way that Amazon lets you know what other people like you have purchased. It's part of making Amazon what Jeff Bezos calls "Earth's most customer-centric company." A few years ago, I experienced what that means beyond the technology.

I've always loved to read great business books, and, back when I lived in New Zealand, I discovered that, even with shipping costs, I had a wider selection and lower prices shopping online at Amazon than at any New Zealand bookseller.

In the days before e-books, I would place an order for about 20 books every three months, and Amazon would send them to me in a box that would arrive within a week. Then, one day, I noticed that a shipment I had ordered two weeks before still had not arrived.

I contacted their customer support. The agent replied by e-mail that, according to their records, the order had indeed been sent and was delivered to my address over a week ago. When we reviewed the shipping address, I realized that I was the problem.

Instead of selecting New Zealand on the online delivery address form, I had selected the next country in the drop-down menu, the African country of Niger. I admitted my (costly) mistake and said I still wanted to purchase the books. I asked them to bill me again and resend the books, but this time to the correct address. That's when Amazon blew me away.

"Mr. Lynch," the agent wrote, "we will give you a full credit for the books you ordered and will send them again to your correct address." I had just been forgiven a mistake of seven hundred dollars! As you can imagine, I've remained a loyal Amazon customer ever since.

Now, which Value Discipline is right for you? Take a moment to think about who your ideal customers are. Think about your company strengths and how your customers think of you.

The basic idea is to compete in a Value Discipline where you can establish a competitive advantage. As Jack Welch advises, "If you don't have a competitive advantage, don't compete." That's the idea behind his successful strategic directive at General Electric – that a GE business should be able to be number one or two in its market. If that was impossible, Welch would sell the business.

Deciding on a Value Discipline sounds like a simple and easy process, but it's very important, and people have strong feelings about it. You need to do the analysis individually and then come together as a group to make your final decision.

You're going to pick a single discipline to be your primary Value Discipline. But that doesn't mean you can ignore the others. Look at the diagram on the next page.

It would be wonderful if you could be excellent at all three Value Disciplines. The problem is that trying to cover them all means that you're spending time and energy and money on things that don't matter the most to your ideal target customers. Instead, I want you to commit to becoming truly excellent at one Value Discipline and good enough at the other two.

"Good enough" means that you match the industry standard in areas that are not your primary Value Discipline. Walmart obsesses about Operational Excellence, but it's good enough on Product Leadership and Customer Intimacy. Apple pours its heart and soul into Product Leadership and matches the competition on Operational Excellence and Customer Intimacy.

Here's how it works for one of my clients, Strategic Consulting Solutions. They provide accounting and compliance solutions for companies in the Southeastern USA who have won government contracts. Their primary Value Discipline is Customer Intimacy. Here's the way they say it:

> We understand the complexities of government contract-
> ing and strive to help our clients find the support solutions
> to all their contracting issues.

They're good enough at the other disciplines. They have experts on compliance and government contract accounting, but they're not "thought leaders" in the field. They aren't the creators of state-of-the-art technology

Figure 6: Choose your Value Discipline

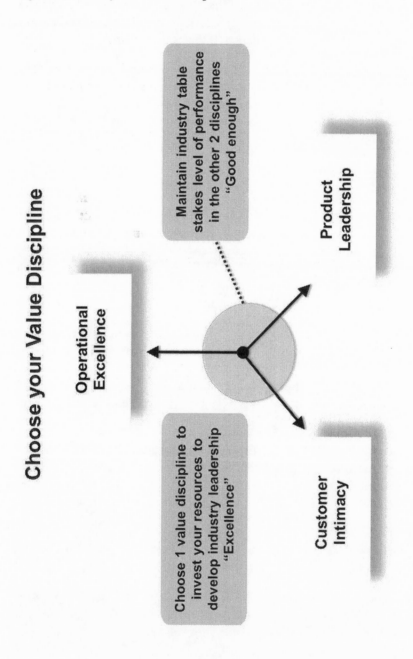

solutions; they leave that to others. They're an efficient company, but so is every other competitive compliance firm. They don't just sell solutions to a market. Instead, Strategic Consulting Solutions puts their time and money and effort into creating the perfect solution for each client.

On the following page is a chart that will help you understand what your strategic focus should be, based on the Value Discipline you choose to excel at.

Ask each individual to make a choice based on the analysis you've done so far. Then come together as a group and work out the decision for your company. What is your chosen Value Discipline?

What Strategic Moves do you need to make now and within the next three to five years to excel at this Value Discipline? Highlight your answers to this last question so we can revisit them later.

When you're ready, turn the page, and we'll begin working on your Core vs. Non-Core Activities.

Figure 7: Your Value Discipline determines your strategic focus

Value Discipline (Generic Strategy)	Strategic Focus
Operational Excellence	**Focus = EFFICIENCY** Consistency, lower cost structure than competitors, cost control, streamlined processes, lower prices, supply chain management, no-frills, large volumes, reliability, speed, replicable at scale, centralization
Product Leadership	**Focus = INNOVATION** State of the art products & services, high investment in research & development, create new categories, performance leadership, brand marketing, speed to market, high margins in short time-frame before fast followers can replicate, continual reinvention
Customer Intimacy	**Focus = EFFECTIVENESS** Deep understanding of customer needs, develop customized products & services, unique solutions, higher prices, close relationships, responsiveness, high-touch customer service, decentralization

Source: Business Execution for RESULTS

Core Versus Non-Core

WHEN I SET MY BHAG of becoming Mr. New Zealand in five years, I knew there were hard things I had to do. I had to follow a strict training and dietary regimen every day. Those were the right things to do so I could achieve my goal.

To get the results you want, you have to do the right things. Everybody tells you that. What you don't hear often enough is that you also have to stop doing anything that isn't the best choice for getting the results you want.

The biggest thing I had to give up was winning competitions. My strategy required that I abstain totally from competing from 1989 to 1992. I needed one long cycle of bulking up and dieting down, and that meant not competing at all for three years. That was very hard for me.

Frankly, I liked competitions – feeling the thrill of victory and standing there on the stage, receiving the applause from the audience. I would have loved winning more trophies and working my way up the rankings, but I had to say no to that experience if I wanted to achieve my goal by the fastest, most efficient route possible. So I sat at the back of the bodybuilding shows every year, muttering under my breath and telling myself to be patient and that my time would come. Saying no to some things was just as important as saying yes to other things. Here are two more examples:

Yes: Heavy weight training

No: Aerobic exercise and other sports like rugby, tennis, swimming, and hiking

Yes: Plenty of rest and recovery, early to bed, and diet soda.

No: Late nights, nightclubs, partying, or alcohol

In other words, achieving my BHAG meant saying no to a lot of things I liked doing but which weren't the fastest route to achieving my goal. In Business Execution for RESULTS, we call those necessary things "Core Activities" and those unnecessary things "Non-Core Activities."

Strategy is making wise choices about what to do and what not to do so that you ensure your future success. The "not to do" part doesn't get discussed that much, but the top experts in creating a winning strategy think it's just as important. Here's Peter Drucker:

> Leaders must decide:
> What is our business?
> What should it be?
> What is not our business?
> What should it not be?

And Jeff Immelt, CEO of General Electric:

> Strategy is resource allocation.
> Strategy means making clear-cut choices about how to compete.
> You cannot be everything to everybody.
> You have to figure out what to say NO to.

And Michael Porter:

> Many managers do not understand the importance of having a clear strategy.
> Strategy is about making trade-offs.
> The essence of strategy is choosing what NOT to do.

You get the idea. Deciding what NOT to do is every bit as important as deciding what to do. That's what this chapter is all about. You'll take a look at what you're doing now as a company and then decide what you should be doing and not doing. When you're done, your activities will be in three groups:

- **Core Activities:** Activities that are necessary to gain strategic advantage and achieve your goal. These are the must-do activities. You want to allocate resources to these activities. If there are Core Activities that you aren't doing now, you must develop them or acquire the capability of developing them.
- **Context Activities**: Activities that you can do effectively in-house, but where you don't need to be superior. A minimum acceptable level is good enough.
- **Non-Core Activities:** Activities you should not be doing at all. If you're doing them now, you need to stop doing them, or out-source them, or divest them. This is, by far, the hardest thing to

do, but it's something that sets great performers apart from the pack. Everything you stop doing frees up time and money and attention for your essential Core Activities.

Start by making a list of everything you do as a company. Include products or services you sell and markets you serve and all the necessary support activities you can think of. Have all members of your team make their own lists, then combine them. Later, you'll sort them into different kinds of activities.

Don't worry about getting this right all at once. Team members should revise their lists as they get ideas. Have a few sessions to combine lists. Stop when you've got a list that isn't changing much from one session to another.

Look at your combined list of activities. Use the flow chart on the next page as a quick overview of how to sort activities into Core, Context, and Non-Core.

Now, go through your list and highlight everything you do that is essential to success, that differentiates you in a meaningful way, and that you're good at. That's your first pass at a list of Core Activities.

Review the activities that are left. Mark everything that's important to helping you achieve your goal using the Value Discipline you selected. If you chose Customer Intimacy, then customer service activities would be important. If you chose Operational Excellence, logistics is usually a key activity. For Product Leadership, product development is core. If you improve the way you carry out these activities, it should have a big impact on your performance.

Let's go back to what's left on your original list. Some of the activities there are necessary for your business to function but are not activities that differentiate you. For instance, keeping records of my food intake was critical for me when I was dieting down in preparation for the Mr. New Zealand bodybuilding title.

I weighed myself every week on the same scale. I measured body fat as well, with the same person and method every time. I weighed every food item I consumed every day, referring to the nutrition almanac to determine the exact number of grams of protein, carbohydrates, and fats and how many

Figure 8: Which activities are really Core?

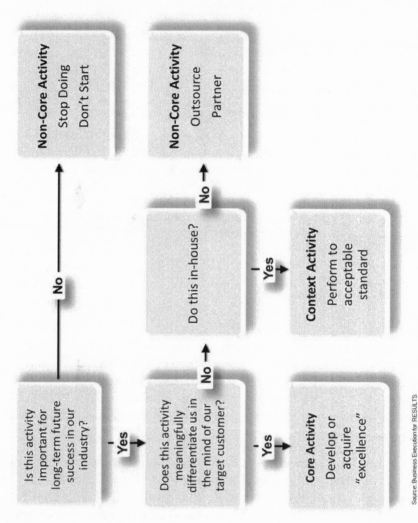

Source: Business Execution for RESULTS

calories I ate daily. I plotted these four data points on a graph every day, and plotted my body weight and body fat on a graph every week. Monitoring my nutrition became a science.

Tracking my food intake was my "accounting" function. Accounting includes a number of activities that are necessary. But no company ever became a market leader because of their accounting. The same is true for most companies when you think about benefits administration or building maintenance. Those are good examples of activities that have to be done, but they're not Core Activities; they're Context Activities. We'll come back to activities like that in a little bit. Now I want you to look at what's left.

What's left are the activities that aren't unique, special abilities you possess and that don't help you stand out from your competition. They're your Non-Core Activities. You should stop doing them.

The hardest things to stop doing are those that aren't part of the new company you're creating but that you've done superbly for a long time. That's when you should read and reread this quote from Peter Drucker:

> There is nothing so useless as doing efficiently that which should not be done at all.

Activities that make money or that could make money can probably be sold off. If you keep them, they'll use up time, resources, and attention you should use for Core Activities. It's tough to get rid of these Non-Core Activities, but it's essential if you want to be your best. Don't wait. Avoid the trap of hanging on to non-essential activities too long.

I know this is hard. It works against human nature. We like to stay with the familiar and, especially, with pursuits that made us successful in the past. But you have to eliminate those activities if you want to seize the future. I'm going to bring in the experts to underline this. First, here's Philip Kotler:

> Long term is NOT about performance improvement. It is about forgetting the past and reshaping the business to compete more effectively in the future.

And Gary Hamel:

> The single biggest reason businesses fail is that they overinvest in what is.

And Peter Drucker:

> Yesterday's star product may produce profits now, but it soon becomes a barrier to the introduction and success of tomorrow's breadwinner. One should, therefore, abandon yesterday's breadwinner before one really wants to, let alone before one has to. Of course innovation is risky. But defending yesterday is far more risky than making tomorrow.

Go through your list and resolve what to do with every item that won't accelerate your success in the future. Decide what to simply abandon. Decide what you will divest or sell.

This is the point where many companies suggest that we should look for cash cows to milk. That's a reference to the famous Boston Consulting Group (BCG) matrix that includes the box labeled "Cash Cow." A Cash Cow is a business that owns high market share in a slow-growing industry.

BCG recommends that you milk that Cash Cow to provide funds for other growing operations. I disagree. The Cash Cow theory looks great on paper but doesn't work out in most companies.

Even mature businesses are rarely stable for long, and they require constant investment of management time and money. Most important, they give you one more thing to pay attention to instead of your Core Activities and key Strategic Moves. That's a temptation, not a good strategy. Heed this warning from Peter Drucker:

> The temptation of business is always to feed yesterday and starve tomorrow.

Keep that in mind as you work through this chapter, but don't stop there. Make it part of the way you conduct your business. You should review your activities every year to identify things you should stop doing. Jim Collins calls this making a "Stop Doing List." Peter Drucker originally referred to the process as "purposeful abandonment."

Now you're ready to look at your lists. Start with the list of Core, differentiating activities. Are there any activities that should be there, but that you're not doing now? You will need to add that capability or acquire it. These activities must be inside your walls if you want to achieve your BHAG.

You have two choices with activities that don't differentiate you or don't give you competitive advantage, but which are necessary to run the company: You can do them in-house, or you can outsource them.

If you decide to handle these activities yourself, you need to perform to a minimum acceptable standard. These activities should be done well, but they shouldn't receive the same attention, effort, and investment as Core Activities. These are your Context Activities.

Outsourcing has been a popular tactic since General Electric outsourced some activities to India in the 1990s. Pick any business process, and you'll probably be able to find a company that's outsourcing it. But many do it for the wrong reasons.

Most companies understand outsourcing as a way to cut costs. That can get you in trouble in two ways: First, the cost "savings" may not be real, especially when you account for shipping delays, communication errors, or service failures. Second, the risk of poor performance goes up when you don't directly control an activity. Dell learned about that first-hand.

Dell is an Operational Excellence company, so there was logic behind their decision to reduce expenses by outsourcing customer service for their computers. In fact, they were among the first computer companies to outsource customer service.

They did save money on their customer service operations, but the move created lots of problems. Customer service complaints tripled. Dell brought back some customer support functions, but then faced the task of rehiring support techs who were fired when service was outsourced. The net result was that Dell wound up losing customers and goodwill.

Follow Peter Drucker's advice: "Your aim is to enhance effectiveness, not to try to lower expenses. Outsourcing, properly executed, might even increase costs." Make the decision about whether to outsource an activity based on your company, your situation, and your strategy. Every company will do things differently.

Both Apple and W.L. Gore are Product Leadership companies. For Apple, product development is a Core Activity carried out by a small group at headquarters. Manufacturing is a Non-Core Activity, so they decided to outsource it. W.L. Gore has a different success model.

W.L. Gore is best known as the developer of waterproof, breathable Gore-Tex fabrics. At W.L. Gore, product development and innovation are activities in which everyone participates. They generate product leadership through a system that gives product champions everything they need to succeed, except formal support. They have to win support by enrolling volunteers to help them with a project.

There's another way in which Gore differs from Apple: At Gore, they see the manufacturing process as a key source of innovation. So the company clusters manufacturing facilities, making it easy for people to run into each other and exchange ideas. Design and engineering expertise is within walking distance of the factory floor. W.L. Gore defines manufacturing as a Core Activity, so outsourcing is not an option, even if it would create cost savings on paper.

Use the chart on the following page as a template: In the left hand column, list your Core Activities, those things in which you demonstrate special abilities and which differentiate you in the mind of your target customer. Look at this over two different time periods: What are your Core Activities now, and, down at the bottom left, what activities will be Core within the next three to five years?

Think about what could change in the coming years. Activities can shift over time into different columns based on the strategic decisions you make.

In the middle column, list Context Activities, those activities that you will perform in-house to the minimum standard. List your Context Activities today and those that will be in that group within three to five years.

Now for the right hand column: This where you need to make some tough decisions. What will you stop doing? You should divest or outsource those activities or maybe even partner with another firm that handles them well. Just stop doing them. Which ones will you stop doing now? Within three to five years?

Figure 9: Where do activities belong?

CORE Activities

Invest resources to perform these "differentiating" activities in a truly excellent manner: Continue doing? Start doing? Develop? Acquire capability?

CONTEXT Activities

"Non differentiating" activities you will perform in-house to a minimum acceptable standard

NON-CORE Activities

Let someone else do it: Not get into at all? Stop doing? Outsource or partner? Divest or sell?

Now?

Within the next 3-5 years?

Source: Business Execution for RESULTS

Business Execution for RESULTS requires courage. These decisions are where you demonstrate true strategic leadership. It is easy to keep adding products and services. It takes real courage to say no. I often say to clients, "You have to constantly prune the rose bush to create beautiful blooms."

That's not easy, and it goes against the grain for many business leaders, but it's one of the keys to creating a winning strategy. We are conditioned to want to fix and grow things. It's hard to pull the plug on endeavors that are no longer working, or pursuits that worked in the past but are not part of the company you need to create to be successful in the future.

You've made key strategic decisions about your Value Discipline and your Core and Non-Core Activities. Next, you'll make some decisions about how you will tell customers and prospects about your company.

Meaningful Marketing

THE DAY I WON THE Mr. New Zealand title, I gave up competitive body-building forever. I enjoyed achieving my big goal, and I learned a lot, but now I was ready for something different.

I had given up police work while I was training, and I had worked as a salesman and spokesperson for a sports nutrition company that sponsored me with supplements as an athlete. Now I was ready for a new challenge, and I wanted to make some money. I decided to go back to university part time to complete my business studies while I worked full time. I continued my extracurricular reading of business and personal development books.

I applied for and got a job with a pharmaceutical company. I started in sales, was promoted to sales manager, then marketing manager, then sales and marketing manager for all of New Zealand. The pharma industry was very good to me. They provided the best training environment a manager could wish for. I got sent all around the world on training courses that taught me how to become a better leader.

My employer also paid for the services of an executive coach, who worked with me every week. In addition to improving my management skills, the experience taught me how coaching can truly accelerate performance improvement.

It was a great job, with a great salary and benefits, plus there was frequent travel to exotic locations all around the world to attend medical conferences and schmooze the medical profession. Then, one morning, it dawned on me – right in the middle of a product launch meeting for our latest wonder drug – that I loved the challenges and the travel and the learning, but I just wasn't passionate about the industry. So I was ready for a change when my best friend made me an offer.

He had lived out one of those dot-com dreams, starting up a business and then cashing out big time. He told me that his next venture would be "goal-setting software" and, because I was heavily into goal setting and personal development, he wanted me to quit my job and work with him. It sounded great, so I said, "Hell, yes!"

Soon I could see that there was a problem. My friend had just spent the last ten years working 20-hour days, eating tuna and rice, and sleeping under his desk before successfully exiting his software business. Now that he was financially free, he felt he deserved some time to enjoy the fruits of his labor. Unfortunately, we spent more time goofing off on the beaches of Majorca in the Mediterranean than we spent developing our goal-setting software. The problem was that I was living off my savings the whole year that we worked on the project, and I realized that if we didn't ship a product and start generating some revenue soon, I was not going to have any savings left.

At about that time I met Simon Mundell, one of the directors of what was then called The Results Group, at an Entrepreneur's Organization dinner. We really hit it off. I told him that my Core Purpose in life is to teach people how to be successful, and he said they did the same thing with businesses.

He knew about my sales and marketing success in the pharmaceutical industry. They needed help building a sales and marketing process for their consulting business and asked me if I would be interested. I said, "Hell, yes!"

The Results Group was full of people who were great management consultants but lousy at selling themselves. I knew I could make a difference there because the company was aligned with my personal Core Purpose. I started out building the sales and marketing function, moved into managing the entire New Zealand team of consultants, and along the way I began working with my own portfolio of client firms. In time, I became a sought-after business consultant myself.

It was the greatest learning and growth experience. The company works with hundreds of new clients every year all around the world, and the consultants share what they've learned with each other. When you do that, your process just gets better and better quickly, because you learn what works and what doesn't in terms of how to grow a business. That's how we refined and improved the consulting model.

We had a business model that worked. And we soon learned something about our competitive environment that would set the stage for some big changes.

For most of the time that people have thought about business leadership and strategy, most of the big ideas have come from the US. Just consider whom we've discussed in this book so far – Boston Consulting Group,

Michael Porter, Philip Kotler, and Doug Hall are all Americans. So are many other great management thinkers like Tom Peters and Ken Blanchard. Peter Drucker was born in Austria but spent his entire career in America. Add to that the fact that the USA is a huge domestic market, and you know why most of the business and personal improvement conferences happen right here.

Every year, I would fly from New Zealand up to the USA for important conferences such as *Fortune* magazine's Business Growth Summit. It was a way to keep up with the latest thinking and cutting-edge ideas. Over the years, I got to see pretty much all the big-name authors and thought leaders and learned directly from the horses' mouths, so to speak. There were always other firms at those conferences that specialized in consulting to small to mid-sized businesses, just as we did.

They assumed that, since I came from a small market like New Zealand, I was managing a small consulting firm, but when I told them how many staff we had (about 70 at the time), their jaws would hit the floor. Usually, I was representing the largest consulting firm in the room. Not only that, no one seemed to have a process that delivered results as well as ours did. My colleagues and I started to think that we could take our consulting business model to North America and be really successful.

It was time to "eat our own dog food": to do ourselves what we help our clients do by putting Business Execution for RESULTS to work. In 2006, we started with a BHAG that (at the time) was: "To be the *world's* leading small business consulting firm."

We started strategizing on how to achieve that goal. We began doing focused and disciplined research on the competition in North America. We analyzed different possible paths to our goal.

It would have been a logical next step to expand to Australia. That would have been logical, but it would have slowed us down.

It was like my plan to win Mr. New Zealand – if I wanted to achieve it in five years, I had to forego winning lesser competitions during that time. Later, in the US, my client AnswerLab chose a similar path, selling to large companies from the beginning, rather than working their way up.

In 2006, the company name was The Results Group. Our competitor research showed that the word "results" was used in the brand names of so many consulting firms around the globe that it was going to be hard to differentiate ourselves using that brand name. We faced an important choice.

We could create and build a completely unique brand name. That would take time and effort, and it would set us apart, but we would face the big challenge of making our unique name known globally. Or we could do something dramatic to own the word "results" and take everyone else using any variant of that name out of play. The bold step we chose was purchasing the RESULTS.com domain. Yes, it cost a lot, but, by owning the domain name, we owned the word "results" in this digital age.

That gave us an excellent brand name, but we still needed a positioning statement. Another word that was very important to us was "execution." In 2006, it was just becoming a common business term, thanks to the book by Larry Bossidy and Ram Charan published a few years earlier. It was perfect for us.

We knew that our consulting process helped our clients succeed because we not only helped them create strategic plans, but we also helped them to implement those plans and deliver measurable results. In other words, we helped them execute the strategy as well as create it. Execution is how strategies deliver results. We positioned ourselves as "The Business Execution Experts."

And we got lucky. Well, "luck" is not really the right term, but it's the only one I've got. The fact is that, if you know your BHAG, all of a sudden your mind spots opportunities that didn't seem to be there before. That's what happened for us.

My colleagues and I kept running into three guys from a boutique Canadian consulting firm when we attended conferences in the US. They served the same type of clients we did. I think we also gravitated to each other because we were the firms from smaller countries in the midst of firms from the US. They said to us, "If you ever come to North America, we'd love to partner with you." After some more research and some negotiation, that's what we decided to do.

On January 2, 2009, Bianca and I got on a plane in Auckland, New Zealand, for our move to Calgary to set up the RESULTS.com operation up there. The temperature was about 80°F (27°C) on a mid-summer's day in Auckland. Later that same day, after 15 hours on a plane, we landed in Calgary. The city was covered in snow, and the temperature hovered around -16°F (-27°C). It was such a shock to the system that I thought Bianca was going to turn right around and fly straight back to Auckland!

I spent 15 months in Calgary, working with our new partners to test our consulting model and adapt it for North American businesses. We also continued to work on our marketing messages and on getting the word out.

On a visit back to New Zealand in 2010, I got verification that our marketing decisions were working. I walked into a restaurant in Auckland and saw an old friend. He waved me over to his table, where he was entertaining a group of clients. "I'd like to introduce you to Stephen," he said. "He is the chief operating officer of RESULTS.com. You know, that business execution company!"

Aha! He did not get the words exactly right, but he got the gist. He knew our brand name and the position we wanted our brand to occupy in the minds of business leaders – that we were "RESULTS.com, the Business Execution Experts."

That's what you're after. You want your ideal target customers (and many others) to know your name and what you do. You've already taken a step toward an effective marketing strategy by defining your ideal target customer in the chapter on Target Market Analysis. You've also selected your Value Discipline, or the way you will deliver value to that customer. You have made decisions around your Core vs. Non-Core Activities. Now you need to define how you will tell your story to your ideal target customer.

Let's clear up one common misconception before we go on: Many people believe that if you have a great product or a great service, you don't need marketing. They like to cite American poet Ralph Waldo Emerson, who supposedly said something like:

> If a man build a better mousetrap, though he live in a cottage, deep in the woods, the world will beat a path to his door.

First of all, the quote is wrong. Here's what Emerson actually said:

> If a man has good corn or wood, or boards, or pigs, to sell, or can make better chairs or knives, crucibles or church organs, than anybody else, you will find a broad hard-beaten road to his house, though it be in the woods.

That sounds great. It seems to imply that if you have a great product or service, you won't need to worry about marketing. But reality is a little different.

Reality is that you can have the greatest product in the world, the most superb service, but, if no one knows about it, you won't have a broad, hard-beaten road to your place. Instead, you will have a warehouse full of excellent products, and you will be sitting around your office, waiting for the phone to ring.

This is where companies make a big mistake with their marketing. They try to market themselves by saying things like: "We've got the best quality, the best product, the best service, the best people." I've got three words for you: waste of time. Yes, all those things are important, but they won't help you be successful with your marketing.

It's not about the product; it's about the positioning. Positioning is what you want your customers to think of when they hear your brand name. Let me give you an example of how this works.

Today, when people buy a wine with the Stag's Leap label from Stag's Leap Winery in the Napa Valley, they expect a fine wine. That wasn't always so. For decades, wine drinkers considered California wines to be inferior to French wines, even though California was producing some excellent wines. When wine drinkers saw the Stag's Leap label, they thought, "American wine? Not so good." That changed in 1976.

That's the year when a British wine merchant organized a blind taste testing that's now often called "The Judgment of Paris." His goal was to prove that the California wines being sold by his competition were decidedly inferior to the French wines that he was selling. Imagine his surprise when tasters reached the opposite conclusion.

Wine experts tasted French Bordeaux from esteemed wineries like Château Mouton-Rothschild and cabernets from California wineries, including Stag's

Leap, and then rated each one. Only the scores of the nine French judges were compiled. At the end of the competition, Stag's Leap's cabernet was judged the very best of the red wines. Other wines from the USA also compared favorably with their French competition.

Overnight, fine restaurants began presenting California wines to their patrons. Sommeliers now thought that American wineries, like Stag's Leap, produced fine wine. But the 1973 Stag's Leap cabernet was the same before and after The Judgment of Paris. The wine hadn't changed; the positioning had changed. Wine drinkers now saw the Stag's Leap label and thought "great wine."

You need to stake out a Strategic Position that will help drive your marketing results. Strategic Positioning is important, and so is your Brand Promise. In the next chapter, we'll cover this in more detail. Right now you need to know about the three dangerous brand temptations.

Companies are tempted to make their marketing cute and complex and sophisticated, even though blunt and simple works best. You'll be more effective if you state your promise bluntly and keep it simple.

Infomercial pioneer Ron Popiel is the master of the blunt and simple promise. Articles about infomercials always play up the scams and almost always use the word "tacky." But Americans spend billions of dollars on products presented on infomercials. In most years, they spend more on those products than they do on movie tickets.

Blunt promises in simple language work for Ron Popiel and for successful marketers in many fields. How about 1-800-GOT-JUNK? Their promise is: "Remove your junk without lifting a finger." That's an example of a blunt, simple Brand Promise.

You're also tempted to ask your customers what kind of new products they want. That sounds so logical, and it works for small improvements, but it's actually a bad idea if you want to be a category leader. W. Edwards Deming points out one reason:

> Asking customers what they want is a systemic flaw. Customers can't say what new product would be desirable three years from today.

That's not the only reason. Doug Hall uses the following quote by Harvard professor Clayton Christensen to highlight one of the dangers:

> An excessive customer focus prevents firms from creating new markets and finding new customers for the products of the future. They unwittingly bypass opportunities.

Let me share one more quote. This one's attributed to Henry Ford:

> If I had asked people what they wanted, they would have said faster horses.

The fact is that the innovations that make you the most profitable are what we call "future-focused" innovation. The best recent example is Apple under Steve Jobs.

There were MP3 players before the iPod, so Apple could have asked MP3-player users what they wanted. And they would have heard some variation on "faster horses." Users tell researchers about the minimal changes to make existing products work better. It was the same for the iPhone and the iPad. In each case, Apple created a new category and led the market, giving customers products with new features that they didn't even know they wanted. That gave Apple huge profits.

Doug Hall reports on studies comparing future-focused innovation with customer-focused innovation in his book, *Jumpstart Your Marketing Brain*. In one study of over 300 companies, researchers found that customer-focused innovation "significantly reduced the uniqueness of new products created." In another study of 120 business units, a future-focused innovation strategy resulted in ten times more innovation success.

There's one more temptation that you have to resist: It often seems like a good idea to offer the customer more choices. That works if there are a limited number of choices and they all reinforce the brand.

Red Bull is the most popular energy drink in the USA and in the world. When you hear "Red Bull," your mind connects it with "energy drink." That's good. Red Bull Energy Shots is a version of Red Bull in a small container with no carbonation and no need for refrigeration. People who know the product still think of it as an "energy drink." That's good, too. Now what about these?

- Coors Mineral Water
- Life Savers Soda
- Fritos Lemonade
- Bic Underwear

Those just don't seem right, do they? Coors is a brand of beer, Life Savers is a type of candy, Fritos is known for snacks, and Bic makes lighters. Yet every one of those "brand extension" products was tried, and every one of them failed.

Al Ries could have predicted that. Ries is an advertising legend and the author or co-author of more than a dozen books on marketing. He and Jack Trout created the concept of "positioning" in their 1980 book, *Positioning: The Battle for Your Mind*. He's devoted an entire book to the idea that "a narrower focus is an advantage."

Once you've narrowed your focus, you have to tell your story in ways that attract new customers and keep the current customers coming back. You do that with simple, straightforward Strategic Positioning. Forget the hype. Forget the gimmicks. Tell your story in a way that people know what to expect from you.

Don't stop with no-b.s. simplicity. Tell the truth and provide proof of your claims. You're living in a world where more than 90 percent of Americans simply don't believe advertising claims. So you must have a strong, truthful, proof-supported message that you repeat over and over.

Advertisers have known for decades that people won't remember you if they only hear your message once. You have to repeat it again and again for the message to be heard and even more if you want people to remember it.

In the next three chapters, you'll take the principles we outlined in this chapter and use a disciplined process designed to help you create a winning marketing strategy that delivers results. Follow the same practice that you have in earlier chapters: Have each member of your planning team answer the questions on his or her own. Then get together as a group to hammer out your final choices and statements.

The decisions you will make in this section are raw concepts that can then be used to brief a branding or design team where necessary. How your marketing strategy is actually executed textually, verbally, visually, and experientially in the marketplace is derived from these key decisions.

We'll start by having you think about your brand name and positioning. Strategic Positioning is the concept you want your customers to think of when they hear your name. This is where you define the way your offering is meaningfully different from your competition's offering.

Ready? Then let's move on and think about your Strategic Positioning.

Strategic Positioning

Strategic Positioning or brand positioning is a statement of who you are. It is what your target customers think about when they hear your brand name. There are two important questions you should answer:

- What word or words do you own in your target customers' minds?
- Where can you be perceived as a leader or as meaningfully different in some way?

Go back and forth between those two questions and refine your answers as you go. As you do that, think about two masters of Strategic Positioning that we've already mentioned.

Red Bull owns the words "energy drink." 1-800-GOT JUNK? owns "junk removal." What words do you want to own? What will make you stand out from the herd?

Seth Godin says that you should stand out from the herd of competitors the way a purple cow would stand out from a herd of cows. That's not just a little different. We're talking "dramatically different," and that takes courage.

The old rule of marketing was that you played it safe. You created a good enough product or service, and then you sold it with PR and advertising. You took out ads, you spent money, and you tried to drive customers to your business that way. That used to work, but it doesn't any more.

Today, you need to create remarkable products or services that your target market customers will seek out and talk about. They will spread word-of-mouth about your brand.

You've already made the critical decisions about how you're going to deliver value to your customer. You chose a Value Discipline. When you made that choice, you had to think about who your ideal target market customers are, and what they currently think of you and your industry. Now it's time to decide how you're going to market yourself to your target market customers.

This is important, because being perceived as dramatically and meaningfully different increases your chances of marketing success fivefold. Remember what happened with Stag's Leap Winery when wine drinkers began to perceive them as an excellent wine?

It starts with being dramatically different. You're either a Purple Cow of a product or service, or you're a commodity. But that's only part of the challenge. You must also be dramatically and meaningfully different to your ideal target market customer. One of the best examples of how this works is an advertising campaign run by Dove, a brand owned by Unilever.

Traditional ad campaigns for what are called "Health and Beauty" products feature young, blemish-free, gorgeous models. They imply that if you use the product, you, too, will appear young and blemish-free and gorgeous. The Dove "Real Beauty" campaign was very different.

They showed pictures of older women, for example, and asked you whether you thought they were "Wrinkled or Wonderful?" and "Gray or Gorgeous?" and "Fat or Fabulous?" When they showed the pictures and choices to both men and women, two-thirds of the respondents didn't like the campaign at all. As for choices, two-thirds of the men picked "wrinkled" or "gray" or "fat." In other words, two-thirds of people in the USA would probably not like the campaign or buy Dove soap. Men almost certainly wouldn't buy Dove soap. But those people weren't Dove's ideal target market customer.

Marti Barletta, writing for the website *MarketingProfs*, described the campaign and the results. She says:

> Within six months, sales of Dove's firming products increased 700 percent in Europe, and, in the US, sales for the products featured in the ads increased 600 percent in the first two months of the campaign.

What we're talking about is Strategic Positioning. It's important to have great products and great services. But too many companies delude themselves by thinking, "If people knew how great our products or services are, they'd buy us every time." Well, I've got three words for them and for you: waste of time.

Just being good is not enough. Your competitors are good. Your customers won't even start down the path to buy your product unless they think you're remarkably, distinctively, and meaningfully different. You don't win the marketing battle with the best product or service. You win the marketing battle with Strategic Positioning. So let's think about how you can position your company.

There's no one best way to position your company so you appear distinctively different from your competition. You need to choose a position that sets you apart in a way that appeals to your ideal target market customer. There are six basic ways to achieve that:

Position your company based on price point. Walmart, for example, offers "everyday low prices." Price positioning can work the other way, too, when people use a high price as an indicator of high value. Consider this story told by Dr. Robert Cialdini, the author of *Influence: The Psychology of Persuasion*.

The owner of a jewelry store that specializes in Indian jewelry purchased some good quality turquoise pieces and priced them reasonably, based on her experience. But, even though the store was full of tourists, those pieces didn't sell. That happens in retail.

The store owner did what store owners have probably done since the beginning of commerce. The night before she left on a buying trip, she wrote a note to her staff, directing them to display the turquoise pieces prominently and to cut the selling price in half. She imagined that customers would snap up the jewelry at the low price and she could move on to other things.

When she returned from her trip, she was pleased to note that, as she expected, the pieces had all been sold. Then she discovered that her staff had not done what she had asked. Her assistant misread the note, and, instead of cutting the prices by half, the assistant had doubled them. The jewelry sold better when the higher prices sent the message to customers that the pieces were of higher quality. There are many stories like this that marketers tell each other.

One of the most commonly told stories is the one about how Chivas Regal was a struggling brand of Scotch whiskey until they doubled their price; according to this account, unit sales doubled. You may have heard the story yourself.

I've used the "Chivas Regal Effect" story for years, and I'm not the only one. It's referred to on websites, in sober magazines like *Time*, and even in marketing books. But none of those "sources" gives any details.

I believe that it's important to get the details right, so I went hunting for them. I thought I had them when I found a footnote in one of Dr. Cialdini's books that referenced the effect. So I followed the footnote to the source, a 1991 book by David Aaker titled *Managing Brand Equity*. Here's the full quote from Aaker's book:

> The classic story is that Chivas Regal had been a struggling brand until its managers decided to raise its price to a level far above its competitors. Sales skyrocketed, even though nothing was changed in the product itself.

Again, no details. It's true that Chivas's sales increased dramatically in the 1950s, but I think the increase could have also been caused by other factors that didn't have anything to do with price: Seagram's bought Chivas in 1949, and they increased the marketing budget and added distribution muscle. And Chivas was Frank Sinatra's favorite Scotch, adding the kind of glamour that sells high-priced products.

That doesn't change the effectiveness of using price to position your product or service, but it does offer a lesson about digging for the facts behind statements that "everybody knows."

Let's look at some other ways you can position yourself:

Position your company by creating a new category. That's what Red Bull did. Before them, there was no "energy drink" category.

Position your company as something different from the category leader. In rental cars, the classic Avis advertising campaign, "We're number two, so we try harder," is a great example.

Position your company as a specialist. 1-800-GOT-JUNK? is the specialist in junk removal. There are coffee shops all over the USA that sell coffee and a host of other things like hamburgers and breakfast and pie, but Starbucks positioned itself as the coffee specialist, the brand you know offers premium coffee.

Position your company as the master of a distribution channel. L'eggs was the first supermarket pantyhose brand and became the largest-selling pantyhose brand in the country. Paul Mitchell became a $600-million hair and skincare brand by focusing on the professional hair salon channel. Ping did the same in golf clubs by focusing on the pro-shop channel.

Position your company by being explicit about who your target market customer is. Curves is the gym solely for women. AXE (or Lynx, in some countries) cologne positions itself as the cologne that makes young men irresistible.

Here are two questions that I recommend to help you identify your Strategic Position:

- In what area(s) could you be perceived as the leader of a category or niche in your industry?
- In what area(s) could you be perceived as being dramatically and meaningfully different from your competitors?

Strategic Positioning doesn't happen in a vacuum. You have to consider where you are positioned compared to your competition. That means returning to the industry analysis to identify your key competitors, looking at their marketing material, and figuring out what positions your competitors have staked out in the marketplace. Answer the following questions so that you have their positions fresh in your mind when you consider your own position:

- Who are your key competitors?
- What strategic position do they claim to own (if any) in their marketing messages?

Now step back for a minute and answer a concept question from the book *Blue Ocean Strategy* by W. Chan Kim and Renée Mauborgne. They are professors at the INSEAD business school who studied 150 Strategic Moves in 30 industries over a century. They define a "Blue Ocean Strategy" this way:

> The aim of a Blue Ocean Strategy is not to outperform the competition in the existing industry, but to create new market space or a blue ocean, thereby making the competition irrelevant.

Is there some open ocean, a bit of blue water, that you can claim as your own?

When you've done your analysis, it's time to state your Strategic Position. A Strategic Position is a statement of who you are. Ideally it conveys leadership or a point of difference. Write it out as best you can. Then refine it into a short phrase. RESULTS.com are "the business execution experts." Who are you?

Remember my Twitter Rule? See if you can state your Strategic Position in a short, concise statement of 140 characters or less.

Now here's a challenge for you: Try the Seth Godin test. State your Strategic Position in eight words or less. Seth maintains that if you can't state your position in eight words or less, you really don't have a position.

At this point, you've analyzed your marketing from your perspective. You've defined who your ideal target market customer is. You've just decided how you want to position your brand relative to the competition.

That's great, but it's not nearly enough. The next big step in Business Execution for RESULTS is to look at things from your customers' point of view and decide what benefits those customers should expect when they buy your product or service.

Key Benefits

Here's a classic marketing story that I love. It's about an elderly woman who needs to buy a new furnace to replace the one in her home that has just failed. Naturally, she goes to an appliance store. There's only one salesman on the floor, so she waits patiently for him to complete a phone call. Then he walks over and introduces himself.

"Hi, I'm Tom. What brings you here today?"

The woman tells Tom that her furnace has failed and she needs a new one. Tom asks her some questions about the size of her home and about the furnace that she has now. Then he launches into a sales presentation.

He tells her something about the makers of the furnace he recommends, their long and illustrious history, and how high they rank in customer satisfaction. He describes the unique features of the furnace, including its operational efficiency and the number of BTUs (British Thermal Units) generated. When he pauses, the old woman speaks up.

"That's very nice," she says, "but will it keep an old lady warm?"

Tom, the salesperson, described features. That's what most of us do naturally. We describe the features of the product or service; we describe the features of our company. We love that stuff, but customers don't care about it. Customers want to know what difference our product or service will make in their lives. They want to know if our furnace will keep an old lady warm.

Features are facts about your brand. Benefits are what these things mean for your customer. "Keeping an old lady warm" is a benefit.

Most companies sell features, but people buy benefits. Great marketing sells benefits. The benefits you provide will also be at the core of your Brand Promise. To deliver benefits that matter, you must go back to your analysis of your ideal target customer so you can understand what he or she wants to buy.

Start by answering the following questions about your customer. Look back at the work you did on Target Market Analysis for help.

- What are your ideal target customers trying to achieve?
- What is the job they want to get done?
- What's their biggest problem?
- What's their biggest frustration?
- What's their greatest desire?
- How does your offering make them feel?

Keep this nearby as we go through the work to define your key benefits. Your key benefits should be relevant and compelling. When you deliver on those benefits, you create superior value. There are three kinds of benefits you can use to create that value:

Functional benefits describe what your product or service does for your customers. These are your offering's attributes, or "the job to be done."

Economic benefits describe what your product or service means to your customers in terms of time or money. Economic benefits appeal to your customer's head, his or her rational part.

Emotional benefits describe the way your product or service makes the customer feel. Emotional benefits appeal to your customer's heart, which is why they are the most powerful benefits.

Most companies can come up with functional benefits quite easily. They are derived directly from features, and that's why so many companies make functional benefits the core of their marketing. However, functional benefits tend to be generic to the category – all your competitors can say essentially the same thing. This is a bad idea for two reasons:

First, the old lady has a job to be done: She wants to know if your furnace will keep her warm on a cold night. Yes, that is what she wants, but focusing on that functional benefit in your marketing is not that helpful, because all furnace brands can claim that exact same attribute, so it does not differentiate your brand in any way.

Second, concentrating on functional benefits can lead to an "arms race" in an industry. I experienced a perfect example when I was in the bodybuilding phase of my life. As I've mentioned, weight gain by adding lots of muscle mass in the off-season is important for every bodybuilder. Protein shakes were an important tool to aid weight gain.

The arms race kicked off when one company claimed that its protein shake would deliver 1,500 calories per serving. That's impressive, but it was only the start. Soon, another company offered a shake that delivered 1,850 calories. Another soon claimed 2,000 calories, and the race was on. Next was 2,700 calories, then 3,000, then 4,000; finally, one of the competitors claimed 5,000 calories.

Car companies spend millions of dollars making this marketing mistake all the time. They talk about how much more powerful or economical their cars are compared to the competition. Computer companies talk about how fast and powerful their processors are. It's not a sustainable marketing claim, and it just keeps the leapfrogging arms race going.

It's essential for your customers to know what your product or service does for them, so functional benefits are important. But they're frightfully easy to copy, so there's no sustainable advantage created.

What about economic benefits? You provide an economic benefit if you give people more value for their money. You can do that by reducing the price. That's how most companies do it. But you can also do it by offering a comparable or better product at the same price, or by decreasing the overall lifetime cost of ownership. Or you can help your customer to be more efficient.

Another way to deliver economic value is to save people time. Many people today will tell you that they need time more than they need money. Remember Tesco and the harried housewife at the center of its marketing bull's-eye? The economic benefit that Tesco delivers isn't in the prices it charges, but in the time it saves consumers, so they can spend less time in the store and more time doing something else.

Economic benefits are more powerful than functional benefits because they consider your product or service from the customer's viewpoint. Economic benefits are important, sure, but ultimately, both functional and economic benefits are easy to copy, and they appeal to the head. Many businesses identify their key functional and economic benefits, call them "the value proposition," and think that their marketing stops there. No, it doesn't.

The most powerful benefits appeal to the heart. Emotional benefits are the way your product or service makes your customer feel. That's what customers are really buying, the way your product or service makes them feel. Jim Stengel, a former marketing manager at Procter & Gamble, puts it this way:

> The modern brand doesn't seek to own a single attribute; it seeks to own a single attitude.

Think about the most powerful brands you know. They all offer powerful emotional benefits.

Harley-Davidson motorcycle riders have such a strong emotional connection with their brand that some have "Harley-Davidson" tattooed on their bodies. The emotional benefit for Harley riders is all about the rebellion and freedom they feel when they associate with the brand.

For years, Harley-Davidson's CEO argued that they sold an experience and that the bike just happens to be a fundamental part of that experience. One of their execs is quoted as saying "What we sell is the ability for a 43-year-old accountant to dress in black leather, ride through small towns, and have people be afraid of him." That benefit isn't a function of horsepower. It doesn't matter if Harley manufactures the most or least sophisticated motorcycles on the road (functional benefit). It also doesn't matter if they are the most expensive or the best-value motorcycles on the road (economic benefit). They give their customers an emotional benefit that can't be easily copied. They appeal to the "rebel archetype" and let you express your inner rebel.

How about AXE (Lynx) deodorant? They're not saying that their deodorant stops more perspiration than other deodorants (functional benefit). They're not saying that their deodorant is cheaper or lasts longer (economic benefit). AXE sells young men the emotional benefit of "use this product and women will find you irresistible." That's powerful stuff.

An emotional benefit can deliver commanding business and marketing results. If you can "own" an emotional benefit in the mind of your ideal target market customers, you can potentially charge a sustainable price premium. You can have a sustainable difference that you won't need to change frequently, even if some details of your product or service change or evolve over time.

With that background, it's time for you to go to work. Start by listing all the benefits your product or service provides.

List all your functional benefits: the service your brand performs, the job it does for your customers, and the attributes of the product or service itself. Functional benefits include what your brand does for your customers – its performance, ease of use, reliability, flexibility, and many other attributes.

Now, I want you to list all your economic benefits. Economic benefits deliver economic value, which means they help people get more for less time and money. Some kinds of economic benefits are lifetime cost of ownership, speed or convenience, responsiveness, time savings, lower error rate, higher productivity, return on investment, and many others.

Finally, list all your emotional benefits. How does your product or service make your customers feel? Emotional benefits include things like feeling in control, safe, secure, clever, powerful, stylish, relaxed, pampered, loved, rebellious, caring, cared for, heroic, adventurous, sexy, fun, sophisticated, prudent, free, belonging, peace of mind, and many others.

We've got one more thing to do before moving on. You need to identify your number-one benefit in each of these three categories. Choose your number-one functional benefit, your number-one economic benefit, and your number-one emotional benefit. These three Key Benefits will form the foundation that supports your Brand Promise.

When you're ready, turn the page. In the next chapter, you'll bring your Key Benefits together with a powerful Brand Promise that will deliver Business Execution for RESULTS.

Brand Promise

Your Brand Promise is the blunt, overt, compelling offer you're going to put in front of your target market customers. Your Brand Promise is going to be derived from, and supported by, your three Key Benefits.

When I think of a Brand Promise, I think of a fly fisherman casting the fly out, trying to get the fish to take the bait. That is what a Brand Promise is. It captures the attention of your target market customers and makes them take action. Here are some standards for your Brand Promise:

You've identified three Key Benefits and a host of other benefits, but your Brand Promise should ideally concentrate on only one benefit – two at most. The success of your Brand Promise starts to drop dramatically if you use more than two benefits as bait.

Your Brand Promise should be blunt and overt. This is not a time for cuteness or what some businesspeople think is humor or creativity. You're 75 percent more likely to be successful if you state your promise bluntly and clearly.

1-800-GOT-JUNK? does a great job: "Remove your junk without lifting a finger." They even managed to combine a functional benefit ("remove your junk") and an economic benefit ("without lifting a finger") into their promise.

You will not attract people who read your promise, understand it, and decide it's not for them. That's OK. What's not OK is if a target market prospect doesn't understand the promise you are making and walks on by, not realizing that you have the perfect solution for them.

Write your Brand Promise in simple language – a twelve-year-old should be able to read and understand it. To get an idea of what that is, check out the late-night TV infomercials for examples of companies that have tested extensively and figured out precisely how to clearly state a Brand Promise in order to get people to pick up the phone and buy.

Remember this quote that's attributed to Albert Einstein: "If you can't explain it simply, you don't understand it well enough."

Figure 10: How to find your Brand Promise

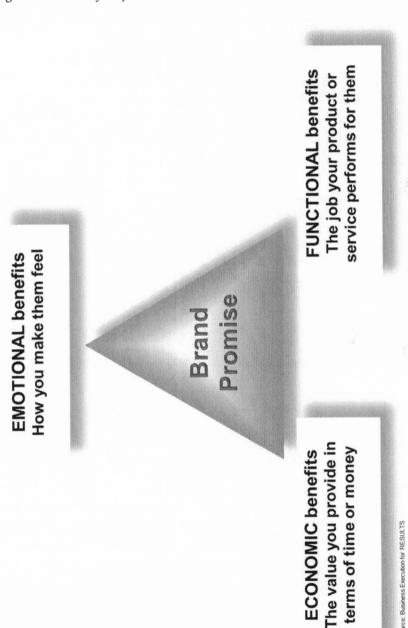

FUNCTIONAL benefits
The job your product or
service performs for them

EMOTIONAL benefits
How you make them feel

Brand
Promise

ECONOMIC benefits
The value you provide in
terms of time or money

Source: Business Execution for RESULTS

Now, let's get to work on your brand purpose. Think about the three Key Benefits that you've identified. What promise or promises could you make to your target market customer?

What promises can you make that won't change, even if your product or service or company changes slightly over time? Look at the 1-800-GOT-JUNK? promise. That promise was good when the company was a small firm in Vancouver, BC. It's good if the service area is all of North America. It's still a good promise even if the company expands the definition of "junk."

Give your Brand Promise some thought. Discuss it with your team. Once you've agreed on a Brand Promise, ask the following questions to test it:

- Is your promise bluntly obvious to your ideal target customer?
- Is your promise something that's hard for the competition to copy operationally?

Work on your promise until you have a short, sweet, clear, blunt statement of your Brand Promise. Your Brand Promise should stretch your company. You company must be structured and optimized to deliver on the promise you make – thus making it something that's hard or impossible for the competition to copy easily. Your promise should be specific, but not too restricting – so that it can grow with you, even if your product or service evolves over time.

Got it? You're not quite done yet.

Why should anyone believe you? This is a skeptical world. Consumers are bombarded by thousands of advertising messages every day, and every one of them includes a promise of some kind. Why should customers believe your Strategic Positioning and Brand Promise?

That's the challenge for every company today. You have to give them reasons to believe.

That begins with telling the truth. No b.s. Tell the truth about your product and what you can do for your customer. If you do tell the truth, you can use several proven methods to provide reasons for people to believe your Strategic Positioning and Brand Promise.

Use demonstrations, so people can see your product in action. Demonstrations are a staple of the infomercial; in fact, they're one of the biggest reasons why infomercials are so successful.

Demonstrations are even more effective if you involve people in providing their own proof. Free trials and test drives are excellent examples of demonstrations that involve customers.

If you have data available, use statistics, surveys, and studies to support your promise. Even your own in-house data can work here. How many customers have you served in the last year? The last ten years?

If your customers tell you that you do a great job, get their permission and share their testimonials. Marketing expert Dr. Robert Cialdini calls testimonials a form of "social proof." Other forms of social proof are case studies and stories of how other people, like your ideal target customer, have used your product or service successfully.

Expert proof is another way to support your Strategic Position and Brand Promise. Obviously, a statement from an expert authority qualifies as expert proof. But so do top ratings from magazines like *Consumer Reports* or rating firms like J. D. Power and Associates, and seals of approval from organizations like Underwriters Laboratories.

Ask yourself this question: "Is there some way we can remove their fear of making a purchase decision?" A guarantee can be a powerful way to do this, and the more dramatic it is and the easier it is for the customer, the more powerful it becomes. Remember that the essence of a guarantee is risk reversal, a message from you to a customer that you're so sure they will get dramatic and meaningful benefits that you will bear the risk.

Before the 2008 recession, Hyundai was seen as a "cheap brand." It was perceived by its competitors as being one of those "inferior products" I wrote about earlier in the section on New Entrants and the Innovator's Dilemma.

In 2009, at the height of people's fears about the impact of the economic recession, this Korean automaker – not historically known for its fearless marketing – paid for a Super Bowl TV commercial that offered the following risk reversal:

Finance or lease any new Hyundai, and if you lose your income in the next year, you can return it with no impact on your credit.

While the car industry suffered a 22 percent drop in sales that year, Hyundai grew its sales 27 percent and increased its market share to become a major mainstream player. *Advertising Age* named it "Marketer of the Year" in 2009. The image of the brand became greatly elevated, to where it is now seen as the equal of the more established brands.

Take a look at the possibilities above and make a list of all the ways you can provide your ideal target market customers with reasons to believe your marketing claims.

Now here's a challenge for you: Can you devise a way to measure how well you deliver on your Brand Promise? Here's how Enterprise Rent-A-Car did the trick.

Andy Taylor is the chairman of Enterprise. He's the son of Jack Taylor, Enterprise's founder, but he wasn't just handed the company. He had to earn it.

Andy started washing cars at a branch when he was sixteen. After college, he went to work at another company, to prove he could make it on his own. Then he returned to Enterprise and started out like every other management trainee, doing all the jobs in a branch. That experience gave him a gut feel for the business that would come in handy later.

In the early 1990s, Enterprise became the biggest car rental company in the US. When a reporter asked Andy about that, here's what he said:

> We are now the largest car rental company in North America, but, really, that's not what we set out to be. We've always just wanted to be the best – by providing a great customer service.

But Andy's gut told him that there were problems with customer service. No one else in the company seemed to agree. Enterprise had been growing rapidly for over ten years, and the other executives didn't want to rock a successful boat.

Andy decided to send out customer surveys to see if he was right. He put together a team of executives to help. The first surveys used several questions to gauge customer satisfaction, region by region. The first results confirmed Andy's guess. Customers were still showing up at Enterprise, but an awful lot of them weren't happy about their rental experience.

A great rental experience was Enterprise's core Brand Promise. They captured their promise with their slogan: "We'll pick you up." No other rental car company did that, and customers liked it. But if customers didn't like the entire rental experience, Enterprise would be in big trouble.

Andy knew that things had to change. He thought that Enterprise should measure customer service so that they could make sure that they were delivering it and could reward the branch managers who did the best job of delivering on their Brand Promise.

He changed the survey so that it measured customer service for every branch and tied branch manager compensation to survey results. He also made it clear that giving good customer service was a requirement for promotion. The customer service score was added to the monthly performance report. Then he and his team simplified the questionnaire.

They discovered that one of their questions accounted for 86 percent of the variation in repeat business and referrals. That question asked if the customer was "completely satisfied with their Enterprise experience." They reduced the survey to include just that question and one more: "How likely are you to return to Enterprise?"

Enterprise uses telephone surveys, so they get results quickly. Quick results mean that Enterprise can catch problems early and have a chance of salvaging relationships that are starting to go bad. The survey taker asks the customer the two questions. If the answer to either one of the survey questions indicates a problem, the survey taker asks if the customer will take a call from the branch to discuss any issues. If the customer agrees, the branch manager gets an email. He or she is expected to follow up immediately.

The system is called the Enterprise Service Quality Index (ESQi). It's powerful because it links operations to the company's Brand Promise.

Your Strategic Position is a statement of who you are. Your Brand Promise should tell your customer what they can expect to receive from your brand. Once you've defined your Brand Promise, follow Enterprise's example. Develop a way to measure it quickly and simply. If appropriate, tie it to compensation.

Remember, the decisions you make in these marketing chapters are raw concepts that can then be used to brief a branding or design team where necessary. How your marketing strategy is actually executed textually, verbally, visually, and experientially in the marketplace is derived from these key decisions.

You've made some key strategic decisions in this section that bring you closer to achieving Business Execution for RESULTS. You've chosen a Value Discipline and identified your Core and Non-Core Activities. You've made some marketing decisions and crafted a Strategic Positioning statement and a potent Brand Promise.

The key analysis and strategic choices are now done, and it's time to swing into action. Turn the page and get started.

GETTING READY TO RUN

Introduction

You know the moment. You know it if you've ever stood on a diving board before your first dive. It's the moment just before you begin something important.

Many companies show up at our door ready to swing into action and "start doing stuff." They don't want to "waste time" on the kind of analysis and decision making you've just completed. They're anxious to start running as fast as they can, as soon as they can. The problem is that they don't know which direction they should run in. They could be headed down a blind alley.

I refuse to help any client run very fast down a blind alley. To avoid blind alleys, you need to make wise strategic choices. Business Execution for RESULTS begins by getting clear on which direction you'll run in.

You shouldn't choose that direction at random. Choose your direction based on a rigorous analysis and decision-making process. Then choose the key strategic moves that will be highly likely to generate the results you want in the future. Only then are you ready to "start doing stuff."

That's where you are now. You've done your homework. It is time to get clear on what we call your "3 to 5 Year Strategic Moves" so you can run as fast as possible in your chosen direction.

You know what your BHAG is. You've done all the basic analysis. You've considered your company and the competition. You've analyzed the market and the state of the world. Now you're ready to take the plunge.

You need to start by reviewing all the potential Strategic Moves you've highlighted in the work we have done so far. That will feel really good, but there's a catch.

You'll discover that you have listed far more Strategic Moves than you could possibly accomplish. You cannot do everything, so some culling will be required. That's hard.

You'll also discover that you have made some contradictory choices and statements in your earlier analysis. That's normal, but you need to reconcile the contradictions before you make your final wise choices. That's hard, too.

What we need to do now is pick the Big Three long-term moves that will guide all your other choices. This is what many commentators consider strategy. I think it's just the start. Strategy includes the wise long-term choices you make *and* the actions you take based on those choices.

Very few companies have done the disciplined preparation you've done so far, so very few are prepared to make choices as wise as the ones you can make. But, once you've made your choices, it's time to step back and see if all those choices make sense when we put them together.

That's what the "Reality Check" chapter is for. We're going to do a SWOT analysis. You probably know that those letters stand for Strengths, Weaknesses, Opportunities, and Threats. Most strategic planners do this at the start of the process. That's a mistake.

If you do a SWOT analysis too early, there's no context, so you can't properly assess the factors. Context makes all the difference. If I ask you if you're ready to take a trip, you won't be able to answer until you know what kind of trip I'm talking about. Where you're going and how long you may stay and whether it's safe and who you're travelling with all have an impact on your answer.

In bodybuilding, you can't assess a training and diet regimen unless you know the goal and how you will achieve it. In business, you can't assess your current strengths, weaknesses, opportunities, and threats until you know the goal and how you're going to get there. You've done a lot of hard work, and you've developed ideas about what will work and not work. In the Reality Check chapter, you will make sure that all those pieces fit together.

The final chapter in this section is titled "What Should We Do Now?"

because that's the question you have to answer. What should you do right here, right now, in the next three months, to start moving forward in your chosen strategic direction? You will decide on the three most important Strategic Projects for you to implement over the next quarter.

If you're like most of the companies that I work with, you're chomping at the bit, leaning forward, and ready to get started. So I know that you're ready to turn the page to the chapter on Key Strategic Moves.

Key Strategic Moves

Sometime in 1988, I got to the point where I had to make some important decisions. I had set my BHAG to become Mr. New Zealand by 1993. I had also done a lot of reading and research and talked to all the experts I could find: pro bodybuilders, elite athletes from other sports, sports physicians, nutritionists, and others. Now it was time to decide what I had to accomplish in the coming years to achieve my goal. You're in a similar position right now.

You've determined your BHAG. You've done a thorough industry analysis and identified your target market customer. You've chosen a Value Discipline and decided what your Core and Non-Core Activities should be. You've made some decisions about how you will market yourself to your customers with your Strategic Position and Brand Promise. Now it's time to put all those things together and make some key decisions about what you need to get done within the next three to five years so that you can set yourself up for future success and accomplish your BHAG. We call these decisions your 3 to 5 Year Strategic Moves. That's what this chapter is about.

I need to make one important point before we go on. Most of the time I want you to follow the advice of Philip Kotler:

> Companies need to operate with one eye focused on the short term and one eye focused on the long term. Short term is about projects related to improving the current core business and meeting the needs of today's target customers.

> The long term is NOT about performance improvement. It is about forgetting the past and reshaping the business to compete more effectively in the future. Often, this demands bold, disruptive strategic moves away from the present to reshape the company for future success.

I want something different in this chapter. I want you to use only your long-term eye. Be patient, we will get to the short-term "right now" stuff very soon. But before we do that, you need to get clear on the long-term strategic direction you should be heading in.

In this chapter, I want you to think about the long term and nothing else. Let's return to Professor Kotler to see what that means. That part about "reshaping the business to compete more effectively in the future" is what this chapter is all about. Many experts think that it's the hardest part of making a strategy work.

Gary Hamel says,

> The single biggest reason companies fail is they overinvest in what is, as opposed to what might be.

Peter Drucker says,

> The temptation of business is always to feed yesterday and starve tomorrow.

Keep that in mind as you think about the future of your company.

The first thing you must do is go back over the work you've done so far:

Your BHAG
Your Industry Analysis
Your Target Market Analysis
Your Ideal Target Customer
Your choice of Value Discipline
Your Core and Non-Core Activities
Your Strategic Positioning and Brand Promise

When you worked on those areas, I asked you at the end of each section to list and highlight the Strategic Moves you should make within the next three to five years to address the issues, opportunities, and threats you identified along the way. I also asked you about the future benefits you will need to offer, the geographies you intend to operate in, and the core competencies you will need to compete in to effectively serve your customers in the future. Pull out those lists now. It's time for you to make some important strategic choices.

I'm going to describe how I do this when I'm working with a client. You should modify the process so that it works for you.

The first thing I usually do is ask my client to go back to the previous exercises and capture all the suggested Strategic Moves that they've come up with so far. Put them on a board or a wall so that everyone can see them.

Before you go on, step back and admire your handiwork. Those suggestions are the result of a lot of hard work. You should feel good about what you've done so far and excited about how that hard work will make a difference for your company. Take a couple of moments to do that before you move on.

When you see all these Strategic Moves in one place, it becomes obvious that you cannot possibly do everything. You have to make some choices about what's most important.

Some of the moves you listed will appear contradictory when placed next to the others. That also requires choices.

Some moves will obviously need to be discarded, because some of your earlier suggestions may not be aligned to the subsequent decisions you made. Eliminate all the moves that clearly no longer make sense. Some may not seem as important now when you see them compared to other moves.

Now, from what's left, you must identify the critical few things, what Dr. Joseph Juran called "the vital few." These are the moves that, if you implement them well, will position your firm for future success in your industry.

These are the big long-term things. You will start working on them now, but they will take a good three to five years, and maybe even longer, to fully play themselves out.

Remember the advice from Jeff Bezos of Amazon.com:

> If everything you do needs to work on a three-year time horizon, then you're competing against a lot of people, but if you're willing to invest on a seven-year time horizon, you're now competing against a fraction of those people, because very few companies are willing to do that. We can't realize our potential as people or as companies unless we plan for the long term.

By extending your time horizon, you lower the amount of competition. Any time you drop down into the "here's what we have to do now," stop and force yourself to pull back and focus with your long-term eye. This is where a consultant can be of great value – to keep you focused on the forest and not the trees, to keep you focused on the destination and not the stone in your shoe that is troubling you right now.

At this point I refer to the advice of Jeff Immelt, the CEO of General Electric. He says,

> Every leader needs to clearly explain the top three things the company is working on. If you can't, you're not leading well.

Your challenge now is to prioritize your list and choose the top three things you must do within the next three to five years to set yourself up for future success in your industry and move you toward achieving your BHAG. Here's how I do that with a client when I'm there in person:

I ask those in the room to vote individually on their top three 3 to 5 Year Strategic Moves. Then everyone goes to the board and marks the items they voted for. Suggested moves that get a vote stay on the board. The others are removed. Sometimes we simply make a separate list of the moves that got a vote.

This leaves you with a much smaller list of things to consider. The team should debate each item that is left and choose the top three, ranked in priority order. That's very easy to say, but it takes a lot of work and, occasionally, some very hot debate.

Don't go on until you have identified the three most important things you must do within the next three to five years and put them in priority order. Congratulations, you are now well on your way to creating a winning strategy. You are well on your way to achieving Business Execution for RESULTS.

There's still one more important thing to do. Yes, you're all responsible for working to make each thing happens, but you also need to make one person accountable for making sure each one gets done.

When you've chosen your 3 to 5 Year Strategic Moves and assigned accountability for each one, then it's time for a Reality Check.

Reality Check

I wanted to be a fighter pilot when I was a young boy growing up in New Zealand. That was my first BHAG. I joined the Air Training Corps as a cadet as soon as I was old enough. I learned to fly solo in a glider when I was in high school. I studied math and physics because I knew you needed that to be a fighter pilot, and, as soon as I was old enough, I applied to join the NZ Air Force.

Here in the USA, you must be a college graduate to become a fighter pilot, but in New Zealand things were different, and I was able to apply at 17. After several weeks of exams and physical assessments, I found myself on the final short list of ten candidates being flown to an air force base in Auckland for the final, grueling three-day selection process.

I was by far the fittest on the course. I found the written exams easy. I was well-prepared, and I knew my stuff. I began to think that I might make it.

New Zealand has a tiny air force. That year, they only selected two people for pilot training. Unfortunately, I wasn't one of them. The examiners told me that I didn't have fast enough reactions to be a successful fighter pilot. That stung; I did not want to believe it. Unfortunately, that was reality. I was good at sports in school. I played in the top teams for tennis and softball in the summer and soccer in the winter. I thought my reactions were one of my strengths, and maybe they were in the context of playing those sports, but in the context of becoming a fighter pilot, my reactions were a weakness. Context is decisive. You need to know where you are heading before you can properly evaluate your strengths and weaknesses.

It didn't matter how big my goal was or how much I wanted it or how hard I was willing to work. I simply didn't have the reactions that a fighter pilot must have. I could have become a navigator, but I realized that even though this was an opportunity, it was not my dream and I wasn't passionate about it.

Now it's time for your version of my air force testing. It's time for you to determine if your goals and plans make sense in the real world, in light of an honest assessment of your capabilities and the current environment. We're going to use a tool that you've probably heard of and maybe even used. It's called SWOT.

SWOT analysis was devised by Albert Humphries, who was at the Stanford Research Institute (now SRI International) in the 1960s and 1970s. Companies still use his basic definitions today:

- **Strengths**: characteristics of the business that give it an advantage
- **Weaknesses**: characteristics that place the company at a disadvantage
- **Opportunities**: external chances to improve performance
- **Threats**: external elements in the environment that could degrade performance

The Wikipedia article on SWOT describes the way most companies and consultants do it:

> Setting the objective should be done after the SWOT analysis has been performed. This would allow achievable goals or objectives to be set for the organization.

In my time in the pharmaceutical industry, I experienced many consultants and strategic planners who were brought in to work with my company. Most tried to start the whole process with SWOT. I thought this was normal at the time, but I've since learned that is a big mistake!

How can you assess your SWOT if you haven't chosen your 3 to 5 Year Strategic Moves and don't know where you're going? You can only assess if you are strong or weak at something in light of where you want to end up. My reactions were quick enough for playing sports. They were strengths in that context. But in a different context, when the goal was to be a fighter pilot, those same reactions were a weakness.

You will assess your strengths and weaknesses in the context of your BHAG and 3 to 5 Year Strategic Moves. Before we start, though, let me remind you of Philip Kotler's concept of dual vision:

> Companies need to operate with one eye focused on the short term and one eye focused on the long term.

> Short term is about projects related to improving the current core business, and meeting the needs of today's target customers.

> Long term is NOT about performance improvement. It
> is about forgetting the past and reshaping the business to
> compete more effectively in the future.

We used the long-term eye in the previous section to determine your 3 to 5 Year Strategic Moves. Now you get to open your short-term eye. This is the skill of great leaders: They are able to keep these two opposing concepts in mind simultaneously.

You need to be very clear on what your 3 to 5 Year Strategic Moves are because you need to prepare your SWOT analysis using those moves as the context. Your SWOT analysis needs to be done with your long-term strategy in mind.

Your SWOT analysis also needs to be done with the current reality in mind. You need to confront the brutal facts in the present. That's what we mean by dual vision. You need to have one eye on the future, one eye on the present, and make sure your SWOT analysis bridges both timeframes.

Here's how I translate that into your challenge in this chapter. Prepare your SWOT analysis in the context of your chosen strategic direction, i.e., the 3 to 5 Year Strategic Moves that you decided on in the last chapter. Your SWOT analysis must also accurately capture your current reality and confront any unpleasant facts.

One way you confront reality is to make it clear and obvious what you're talking about. I've seen too many companies fool themselves by using platitudes and general language.

They tell you (and put in their promotional material) that "our people" or "our brand" or "our culture" are their major strengths. Using that kind of vague, general language is not helpful. Every company seems to want to say these things when I work with them, and I often wonder if it is only to make them feel better about themselves. But is it really true? Can you prove it? You have to dig around inside phrases like that to make what you really mean clear and obvious. You must use specific, concrete language.

What is it about your people that makes them a strength? More specifically, what do they do and what are the results of what they do?

What, specifically, makes your brand a strength? How do you know?

Culture is a very vague term. What are the values and behaviors that define and demonstrate your culture? What are the specific, concrete ways that your culture is a strength?

Get real. Would an outside investor looking at buying into your company agree with you that these are the strengths they are investing in?

Those are just examples. I recommend that you describe each of your SWOT factors in short, concise, three- to five-word descriptive statements.

Context is important here. Identify your strengths, weaknesses, opportunities, and threats based on your BHAG and your 3 to 5 Year Strategic Moves. They are the moves you identified in the last chapter.

This isn't easy, so don't expect it to be. When I work with clients in person to help them achieve Business Execution for RESULTS, this is a place where I have to push and pull and poke and prod them hard. I call them out on any b.s. I am hearing, and I drill down deep to get to the heart of the issues. They find it confrontational at the time, but they come away delighted with the result.

I help them to think differently and take a broader strategic perspective by asking questions like:

- If I were a venture capitalist looking to invest in your firm, assessing your company rationally and dispassionately, what strengths would I be investing in that I can leverage?
- What weaknesses would I uncover that need fixing?
- What future opportunities would I want you to pursue with my investment funds?
- What threats could prevent me from realizing a return on my investment?

Take the time you need to list your strengths, weaknesses, opportunities, and threats ranked in priority order. Most clients start with a list of each. Then they narrow down the list to the top five and rank those five in order.

Here's one way to get the job done: Once you've got your lists, divide into two or four teams, depending on the number of people you've got working on this.

Each team should take one or two letters from the SWOT acronym and make the definitions and statements as clear as they can. Then each team should present their statements to the group. The teams that didn't refine the list for that word should critique the definitions and statements so they get even better.

Remember that your SWOT analysis will set the stage for the actions you'll take in the next quarter. That means you must make sure that everything important is on your lists. Take the time to do it right.

Your SWOT analysis should define your current reality so clearly that a new person in your company, your banker, an investor, or an outside consultant like me should be able to look at your statements and say, "Yes, I get what you mean." To get there, let's review each dimension individually.

Strengths

Your strengths are the assets or the competencies within your current business that you can leverage. What would be your number-one strength as a company? If you could identify one thing that you would say makes you strong, what would it be? What makes you uniquely different in your industry? Remember to assess your strengths in the context of your 3 to 5 Year Strategic Moves and capture them in short, concise, three- to five-word descriptive statements.

What is your number-one strength? If there were two things that make you strong, what would that number-two thing be? If there were three things, what would that number-three be? I'm going to limit you to five. I would like you to list what you think are your top five strengths.

Weaknesses

Weaknesses are next: What are the biggest weaknesses in your current business that you think could be fixed or improved within a 12-month time window? Remember to assess your weaknesses in the context of your 3 to 5 Year Strategic Moves and capture them in short, concise, three- to five-word descriptive statements.

Again, if you could fix only one thing in your business, what would that most important thing be? If you could fix two things, what would be that second most important thing?

Remember that you need to list everything that's important, even if it's something that you don't want to admit or that makes you uncomfortable. That's where I've seen many firms come unstuck.

There is an elephant in the room, and they're not addressing it. The elephant is almost always a weakness or a threat. Often it has something to do with a weakness in their business model concerning sales, future revenues, cash flow, or profitability. Or there is a threat that people may be aware of, but they are not doing anything about it other than "hope it doesn't happen to us." Do you have anything like that? Be brutally honest with yourself. Everything that needs fixing or improving or addressing for you to implement your 3 to 5 Year Strategic Moves should be stated here.

Opportunities

What opportunities can you pursue within the next 12 months? They should be aligned to your future strategic direction, your 3 to 5 Year Strategic Moves. What opportunities can you pursue that will move you in that direction? What can you do now that will position your company for future success? Again, use short, concise, three- to five-word descriptive statements and rank these in priority order. Remember that opportunities are outside your firm. What actions can you take to seize them, exploit them? Rank your top five in priority order.

Threats

What external threats do you need to reduce or closely monitor to ensure they do not derail your plans? If you have done a thorough industry analysis, you should have identified a number of different threats that could impact your industry or your firm. What are they? What are those things, ranked in priority order, that you need to keep an eye on? Which ones should you mitigate, take some action to reduce or eliminate? List the top five threats ranked in order, using short, concise three- to five-word descriptive statements.

You should end up with four lists, one for each letter of your SWOT analysis.

Let's look ahead for just a moment. Your next step will be to take your SWOT analysis and use it as the framework for deciding the important things you must do in the next quarter to move your company in the direction of your 3 to 5 Year Strategic Moves and toward your BHAG.

Let's say you had one of those elephants in the room that I talked about. Maybe it was cash flow, and you decided that was your number-one weakness. To address that, you might decide to implement some initiatives to reduce your total outstanding receivables and your Days Sales Outstanding over the next quarter.

If you succeed, that would change your reality, wouldn't it? While you're working away building on your strengths and making your weaknesses irrelevant, your competition will be busy, too. A new threat may emerge in your industry. New opportunities can pop up, too. That's why your SWOT analysis is never really done.

You should review your SWOT analysis every 90 days. They're "Rolling Reality Checks." That revised analysis becomes the basis for action in the next quarter. That's how you stay agile and effective, and achieve Business Execution for RESULTS.

Now it's time to use the SWOT analysis you've just completed to decide your actions over the next three months. It's time to answer the question: "What should we do now?"

What Should We Do Now?

What should we do now?

That's the question many of you wanted to answer when you picked up Business Execution for RESULTS. In fact, that's where many of you wanted to start. Well, now you're ready to decide what to do now, this week, this month, this quarter. You may have wanted to start sooner, but you weren't ready until now.

Swinging into action without doing a proper, disciplined analysis is like starting to cook without knowing who is coming to your dinner party or without planning the menu. That's how many companies do strategy: They start doing without analyzing, thinking, and planning. When you do that, you lack discipline and focus, which usually means that you go after any opportunity that presents itself.

I call that "chasing after squirrels": Ah, there's a squirrel! Let's go after it! Oops, there's another that looks better. Let's go after that one! Wait, look over there, that one looks even better!

Another common trap with the "just do it" approach is that business leaders can get so focused on improving "what is" (the current business model), that they fail to take action to "create what will be" (to address industry changes and build capabilities for the future).

You shouldn't do that. You've set the context with your BHAG and the disciplined strategic thought process you have been through. You've chosen your 3 to 5 Year Strategic Moves, the things you need to get done within the next three to five years that will move you toward your BHAG. You've tested your ideas with a SWOT analysis to define your current situation in the context of your strategic direction.

Your BHAG and your 3 to 5 Year Strategic Moves are the lenses you look through with your long-term eye. Remember what Professor Kotler says about that:

> Long term is NOT about performance improvement. It is about forgetting the past and reshaping the business to compete more effectively in the future. Often, this

demands bold, disruptive strategic moves away from the present to reshape the company for future success.

Your SWOT analysis is the lens you look through with the short-term eye that Professor Kotler talks about:

> Short term is about projects related to improving the current core business, and meeting the needs of today's target customers.

Now you need to use both eyes as you decide what to do in the next quarter. Just as in real life, you have a richer, more nuanced view of the world with two eyes. This is also the start of a process you will do every quarter. You'll analyze and update your SWOT, which will always be slightly different than it was the quarter before. Then you'll decide your "Strategic Projects" that you need to accomplish in the next quarter to move your business forward.

Take a look at your SWOT analysis again. You've created a list of five items for each element. The items on each list are ranked in priority order. Your current SWOT analysis is like a snapshot of your current competitive situation. You want to work on the things that are at the top of the lists.

In the next quarter, you want to achieve things that will address the key items listed in your SWOT analysis, so that at the end of the quarter, when you redo your SWOT analysis, your situation has improved and you have moved your business forward in your chosen strategic direction. Here's how to think about each element:

Leverage or build on your Strengths. You might want to build on the things you do well, that give you a competitive advantage and that will move you toward your goal. For example, if you're a software developer with a strength in developing mobile apps for financial firms, you might hire more programmers with the skills you need.

Fix or improve the areas where you are Weak. By the end of the quarter, you might want to eliminate a weakness or reduce its impact and drag on your progress. For example, if your cash flow is weak, you might work to reduce your Days Sales Outstanding.

Take advantage of Opportunities. You've identified areas where you can make a major move. You might want to seize one of those opportunities. For example, you might be able to form a partnership with a non-competing company serving the same target market customers that can give you access to their distribution channel.

Mitigate or reduce any Threats. You might want to take action to reduce or mitigate a threat. If a big-box store is expanding into your trading area, you might develop new personalized services that deliver value to your customers. Or, if you're at risk of a power outage fouling up your production schedule, you might invest in backup power generating systems.

You are going to focus on no more than three Strategic Projects to work on in the next three months. Each project should be about addressing an issue in your SWOT analysis and moving you in the direction of your 3 to 5 Year Strategic Moves and toward your BHAG. Use both your short-term eye and long-term eye so your projects achieve a balance between "improving what is" with "creating what will be."

Start with your most important issue. What should you do this quarter to move things forward? We call those things "projects" because they will take several weeks/months to complete.

Most businesses try to do too much, and, as a result, they execute poorly. Your challenge is to identify no more than three issues to address this quarter and define the specific Strategic Projects that will move your company forward. Describe each project in detail. What will you need to do and achieve to make that project a success? What are the important milestones?

Once you have your projects defined, it's time to do two things: First, you will structure your projects in ways that make the project easy to understand and more likely to succeed. Second, you'll test these goals against the reality of doing business every day.

I like the SMART acronym for describing how to structure goals of all kinds, but there are literally dozens of versions of this acronym. One researcher examined 40 websites that used the acronym SMART to define the criteria for goals. When he looked at all the words they used for the different letters, he calculated that it was possible to form almost 9,000 versions of the SMART acronym. The version I use has worked for me and companies I've worked with. It should work for you, too.

In my SMART acronym, the letters stand for Specific, Measureable, Achievable, Relevant, and Time-bound. Here's more about what each letter means:

Specific – You need to state your goal so it is obvious to everyone exactly what needs to be done.

Measureable – It should be obvious when you achieve the goal.

Achievable – You should be able to accomplish the goal by the due date. If you can't, you should probably scale down the goal for this quarter.

Relevant – This is the part of the acronym I see most people get wrong, and it is probably the most important. Many people incorrectly say that "R is Realistic," but, to me, that means exactly the same thing as Achievable. Relevance is what we are looking for here. Is this project relevant? Does it address the current reality listed in your SWOT analysis, and does it move you in the direction of your 3 to 5 Year Strategic Moves and toward your BHAG? A good project should be a short-term improvement, but it should also help you create the future. It must be relevant to your chosen strategy.

Time-bound – The difference between a dream and a goal is that a goal has a deadline.

Each of your Strategic Projects should pass what I call the "Champagne test." That means that it should be so clearly stated that everyone will know when you've achieved the goal and when it's time to pop the cork and celebrate. It's important to celebrate the short-term milestones that you reach every quarter so your people get to experience the thrill of achievement and be acknowledged for it in some way. That helps you maintain momentum and build enthusiasm.

It's like a series of quarterly sprints. You choose the direction you are going to sprint toward your 3 to 5 Year Strategic Moves and BHAG. You set a finish line that you can clearly see. Three months is close enough to see the finish line, yet still enough time to get some significant things accomplished. You put your head down and run. When you get to the end of the quarter, you pick your head up to celebrate how far you have come, assess the current reality again, choose some new short-term Strategic Projects, then put your head down and sprint off again.

Before you go on, take a moment to clearly define the top three Strategic Projects that you can implement within the next three months to address the key issues you have identified in your SWOT analysis.

Some of the projects may take longer than a single quarter to fully implement. If that is the case, define the milestone you intend to reach by quarter's end. Create a specific destination point that you need to reach in 12 weeks' time, and make sure it passes the Champagne test.

You need to be realistic at this point and set yourself up for success. Make sure that you can reach the goals you set in the three months' time that you have.

At this point, many companies write a Strategic Project that ticks off all the letters of the SMART acronym, except for Achievable. They create expectations that would be fine if all they had to do was work on the project, but they don't. Neither do you. You've got a business to run.

The idea is to balance optimism with realism. Remember that you still have to do everything that makes your business go. You have to make sales and fulfill contracts and collect money. You need to do human resources and regulatory paperwork and your taxes. None of that goes away.

Not only that, there will be surprises, things you can't anticipate. "Stuff" happens! Fires will break out, and someone will have to spend time and effort fighting them. That's just the way it is in life and in business.

I've found that it makes sense to set aside one half-day every week when you do nothing but work on your Strategic Projects. That doesn't sound like a lot, but it's realistic for most people in most companies as they try to balance strategic execution with running the business as usual. The trick is making sure you do something every week to make progress on what's important.

Take a moment to look at your Strategic Projects again. Will you be able achieve the milestones you have set by having everyone who is involved working a half-day per week to move them forward? If the answer is no, adjust your expectations and milestone targets to reflect reality. When in doubt, choose to make the project more achievable rather than more ambitious.

Since you won't have a lot of time to devote to your projects, it's especially important that you make some progress every week. Here's how to make sure that happens. This is a powerful technique that I learned from Stephen Covey.

He told a story he called "The Big Rocks of Life." He also demonstrated this principle in his programs. You can probably find a video of it on YouTube if you search for "Big Rocks" and "Covey." I urge you to do that, because the demonstration is so powerful. For now, though, you'll have to make do with my explanation:

The important things in life and work are your big rocks. You also have other things you have to do every week; think of them as gravel. And there are the little things you have to do everyday. That's sand. Now imagine that your challenge is to put as much as possible into a bucket.

Most of us – naturally, it seems – put the sand (daily work) and the gravel (weekly and monthly work) into the container first. We schedule all our routine work and then try to fit the important project work (the big rocks) into an already full schedule. It never works. It seems as though there's never enough time.

The solution is to put the big rocks in first. That's the only way you'll make sure they get into your bucket. You have to schedule the important things first and then fill in around them.

Think of each Strategic Project as a bucket. You must define the big rocks that need to be put in first – that is, what are the major sub-components that need to get done during the quarter to ensure you achieve your Strategic Project milestone by the end of that quarter? These rocks are smaller sub-projects or tasks that you could assign to different individuals – the big things that they need to complete by certain dates to ensure the overall Strategic Project is completed on time.

Then, at the beginning of every week, you figure out the gravel (key tasks for the coming week to move your projects forward). Don't worry about the sand. You will figure that out as you go along.

Schedule your half-day of Strategic Project work in your calendar first. If you use an automated calendar, you may want to make it a recurring appointment. We all know that there will be weeks when you have to re-schedule, but that's the way it is. When that happens, you'll know you're making an exception in scheduling your project work for a different time.

You must have someone accountable for every Strategic Project. Single-point accountability is crucial. If more than one person is accountable, then no one is accountable. Someone's ass must be on the line to make sure it gets done. If that's you, it does not mean you have to do all the work your-self – it means you take accountability to manage the project to success.

Here are the things a project leader should do in order to get the job done. Our clients have proven that it works:

- Meet with each individual who is involved with the project on a weekly basis.
- Review the current status of each person's tasks.
- Make a plan for catching up or getting help if necessary.
- Make sure that each person's number-one task (or next step) to move the project forward each week is agreed and kept visible.
- Report to the company leadership every week on project status and take full accountability for Business Execution for RESULTS.

I suggest you try the following way to manage a project. It's worked for many companies.

In the first week after each quarterly strategic planning session , allow peo-ple one week to research and plan the execution of their individual sub-projects and tasks. Then agree on milestone due dates and "lock in" the dates. Do not alter the due dates after this point. If a project falls overdue, there may be a valid reason, but you must show that the person did not complete their project on time, otherwise it's too easy to let excuses substi-tute for performance.

Get used to this: Every quarter, you'll do your SWOT analysis and then choose your Strategic Projects for the next three months. The key to ex-ecuting your 3 to 5 Year Strategic Moves, achieving your BHAG, and get-ting to the top of your mountain is to continue to assess your situation and make progress every quarter.

One important key to successful Business Execution for RESULTS is to measure performance and track your progress accurately. That's what I'll turn to next. When you're ready, turn the page and begin the section on "Success by the Numbers."

SUCCESS BY THE NUMBERS

Introduction

When I was working toward the goal of being named Mr. New Zealand, I measured several things so that I would know how I was doing. They were my personal Key Performance Indicators (KPIs).

KPIs are important in business. They were important in bodybuilding, too. Unless you are measuring what you are doing every day, it is easy to kid yourself when you are training. To defeat that tendency, I carried a journal and wrote down how many days per week I worked out at the gym. I recorded every set of every exercise I did, how much weight I used, and how many reps I performed.

You may feel like you are working hard and training to the point of failure, but unless you have done at least as many reps as you did the last time you performed that exercise (and preferably one or two more), and unless you have added a couple of extra kilograms to the barbell, you are not actually making progress.

The same is true about diet. You might be climbing the walls with hunger when you're on a pre-contest bodybuilding diet, but unless you are measuring your calories and macronutrients, you may still be eating too much food to achieve your desired body fat percentage by the contest date.

Your brain may be telling you otherwise, but the numbers don't lie. It's easy to kid yourself to think you are making progress when you are not.

In business, measurements and numbers are important, too. We talk about "making your numbers," and we say that "the numbers don't lie." This section is about understanding the numbers that will help you achieve your goals. You'll learn to use the numbers in ways that make a difference in your results and keep you moving forward.

Using numbers to move toward great performance starts with picking the right targets. That's what we'll cover in the chapter on Numerical Targets. The right numbers are numbers that are aligned to your 3 to 5 Year Strategic Moves and that measure your progress toward your BHAG. You also want to choose numbers that everyone in the company understands.

Posting numbers that tell everyone in the company how you're progressing is one powerful way of engaging everyone in the process. You want to share your progress in ways that people can see, understand, and talk about with each other.

You should project your Numerical Targets out over more than one time horizon. That helps people visualize and connect with how your company plans to grow and evolve. It's an important part of the rolling process of Reality Checks and of resetting your Strategic Projects and Numerical Targets. When people observe targets beyond the current quarter, they see their effort in the context of both short- and long-term results.

The chapter on KPIs and Accountability is about identifying the Key Performance Indicators for your company. They are the handful of crucial numbers that measure the daily and weekly activities that drive your business model and financial statement results. These are the numbers you will review in your meetings and track on your dashboard or business execution software. That's important, but not sufficient to drive results.

You must also assign single-point accountability for every KPI. Lots of people may work on a KPI, but one person takes ownership and assumes sole responsibility for performance.

Next, we'll look at a special kind of KPI: Role KPIs. We call this chapter "Organizational Structure and Role KPIs" to indicate that the choices are specific to each of the key functional areas in the business. We need to define what the performance standard is for each role so that we make sure that we have all the operating bases covered for the whole company.

Role KPIs will be slightly different for every company. Industry plays a role. In some, research and development is a key function, but in others it won't be. And Role KPIs are different at different stages in the life of a company.

In the beginning, the founder usually does it all. Later, the company might hire a marketing specialist who's responsible for all marketing. As the company grows, it might add separate people responsible for advertising and public relations. At another growth stage, that same company might have general managers, each with P&L responsibility for a business unit. Every key role that is created must have a KPI that measures successful performance in that role and a single person accountable for performance.

In the final chapter in this section, you'll learn about the critical link between creating strategy and Business Execution for RESULTS. Developing a robust strategy is not enough. You also have to keep important things top of mind so that you take meaningful action on your Strategic Projects every week.

That's what the final chapter is about. You'll learn about tracking and sharing results. I named it "Beyond Dashboards" for two reasons: First, a dashboard is only one way to get the job done, and, second, new generations of business execution software go beyond what the classic dashboard could offer.

Numbers are important in business, but it's not the numbers alone. It's picking the right numbers to track, assigning accountability, and then making the numbers happen. Turn the page and let's get started on setting your Numerical Targets.

Numerical Targets

I must have looked gobsmacked, because I was. My conference luncheon partner was a top human resources executive for a very large company. I asked him how many people worked for his company, and he didn't know. When he saw my amazement, he explained, "Look, we've got a lot of people working for us, about 20,000, in fact. But the exact number doesn't tell me anything, so I don't worry about it. Instead, I pay attention to numbers that matter."

"Like what?" I asked. I always want to hear about how different companies succeed.

He set the context for me first. "We're a manufacturing company, and a lot of our competition is offshore. Our strength is an experienced workforce. Long term, we want to maintain that edge and grow it. Our average day-shift worker has been with us for 14.2 years. I track average tenure, as well as turnover and hours of training."

Business is filled with numbers. There are accounting numbers and numbers that measure operating results, and then there are the ratios and other numbers you can derive from the original ones. You've got lots of choices. This chapter is about the numbers you want everyone in your company to be aware of, understand, and talk about. Let's start with the example of fictional company A.

This company chose "Number of Paying Customers," "Number of Branch Offices," and "Number of Resellers" as the Numerical Targets it wanted everyone to be aware of. You might be asking yourself why it didn't choose a financial measure like sales or revenue per employee.

Not everyone understands or is motivated by hitting financial targets and accounting ratios.

However, everyone – from the most junior employee through to the CEO – understands what a branch office looks like. They also know what a paying customer looks like. Those are tangible things that people can imagine and count for themselves if they wanted to.

The company used the chart on the following page to capture and display its Numerical Targets.

Figure 11: Numerical targets – fictional company A

Choose milestones that have meaning for ALL your people. Must be aligned with your financial forecasts / budgets.

Numerical Target Description	2 years	1 year	90 Days	Person Accountable
Date:	31 Dec 2015	31 Dec 2014	31 Mar 2014	
# Paying Customers	3000	1500	400	Brian
# Branch Offices	4	3	1	Susan
# Resellers	13	8	3	Karl

Source: Business Execution for RESULTS

Everyone in the company knows that the goal is to have a total of 400 paying customers by the end of the current quarter. They know that the goal is to have a total of 1,500 customers by the end of the year. And they can see that, by the end of the following year, the company plans to have 3,000 customers.

Now the employees have something tangible they can visualize and grasp. They know how the company intends to grow and evolve. They can also see that the company intends to open more branch offices to serve these customers, which no doubt means it will be hiring more staff as well. Wow! This company is going places! The future is bright!

Using numbers like this helps employees visualize how their own personal careers could fit into this picture. Perhaps there are future opportunities for them to grow and develop with the company as the company achieves eachmilestone and makes progress toward these Numerical Targets.

Let's consider the principles. You may want to refer to the chart below.

Everyone should understand exactly what the number means. You can track financial results as Numerical Targets, and some companies do. But most people understand visible, concrete things, things they could count if they chose to.

You're going to track these numbers publicly, so select measures that you don't mind sharing. Remember that you want the people in your company to be aware of these numbers and discuss them. Inevitably, the competition will learn what you're tracking, so make sure you don't mind.

The numbers you track should be aligned to your strategy. The rule is simple: strategy first, then numbers. Select numbers that are based on your BHAG, 3 to 5 Year Strategic Moves, and Strategic Projects. These numbers will be the basis for your budgets, financial forecasts, human resource planning, and more. Budgets and forecasts should not be done until you have created your strategy, and they must be aligned to the strategic choices you have made.

Display the numbers over different time periods. The numbers for this quarter are important. They're hard targets, the things you definitely expect to achieve in the next three months. That gives your team clear goals to aim for, but you need to provide some additional context. Based on your Strategic Projects and what you know to be true right now (your current reality), what do you expect to achieve by the end of the current year? What about the year after that?

The further you project into the future, the less certain you can be, because, as we know, your current reality (SWOT) is always changing. Thus, you need to review and update your Numerical Targets at the end of every quarter to ensure your stated goals always reflect the current reality. Nothing is more demoralizing or pointless to your people than keeping annual targets in place that bear no resemblance to the current reality.

Someone must be accountable. There must be a single person who is accountable for achieving every goal.

Now it's time to get to work on Business Execution for RESULTS. Get your team together and do the following:

Choose at least one, but no more than three, Numerical Targets. Make sure they are numbers that have meaning for all your people. Project them over three time periods: 90 days, one year, and two or even three years. Identify the person who's accountable for making those numbers.

Decide how you will make the targets visible. These targets and your progress should be a regular topic of interest and conversation. Make them noticeable and provide frequent progress updates. Some companies use technology to help. I've seen companies use giant computer screens in their offices to display the current numbers and highlight progress in real time.

Each target also has the name of the person responsible for hitting it. For those people, the Numerical Target is not simply something to be aware of; for them, the target is probably the end result of meeting their Key Performance Indicators every week. That's what we'll discuss in the next chapter.

KPIs and Accountability

At the end of every month and quarter and year, your company probably generates a balance sheet and a profit and loss statement. No matter how accurate they are, they're only looking in the rearview mirror.

To improve your results, you need to pay attention to the things that drive the financial results of your current business model. Don't try to pay attention to everything. If you do, then you squander your attention on many things that don't produce much of a result.

Instead, concentrate on the few but important things that make a big difference. We call these your Key Performance Indicators (KPIs). These are the handful of leading indicators that will predict and drive the success of your current business model.

When you've identified your KPIs, you'll be able to say: "If we get these things right, we'll have good results on our financial statements and increase the value of our company." Here's an example from my own experience: Many years ago, when I was a pharmaceutical sales manager, I concentrated on the number of physician visits that my sales reps made every week. I learned that the number of visits was a key driver of financial results. So, every week, I would review the activity records for the salespeople who worked for me.

When you're trying to identify KPIs, you need to go beyond the first answer to find your most important results drivers. So, in this case, it was not "sales" (the eventual outcome) but "sales calls" (the activity that drove the outcome) that was found to be the key. Here are a few more examples:

A professional services firm might use billable hours as a Key Performance Indicator. My friend from HR used training hours. A construction or contracting firm might choose the number of proposals submitted. Another firm might select "backorder percentage" as a KPI. Remember to pick KPIs that drive financial results in your current business model.

KPIs do more than simply measure activity. They send a message to the people in your company, telling them what's important. KPIs tell your staff what you will pay attention to. In other words, KPIs drive behavior. They help align individual priorities with company priorities.

Since all the sales reps I managed knew that I would be monitoring and verifying the number of calls they made with physicians every week, it made a difference in how they worked. If they were tempted to knock off early on a Friday afternoon but had not made their quota of sales presentations, they'd be much more likely to squeeze in a few more sales calls before wrapping up the week. What you pay attention to drives behavior.

Define KPIs that you can measure every day or every week. If your measurement cycle is longer than a week, you don't catch problems early enough. You get better performance with shorter measurement cycles. Shorter cycles let you spot trends earlier.

When I worked as a sales manager, a single week of sales rep appointment data didn't tell me much. A rep might have a high number because he or she was able to group appointments close together in a certain region. Or there might have been a low number because of travel requirements to service that region.

But with a weekly cycle I could quickly identify the patterns. If a rep had two weeks in a row with below-standard call numbers, I needed to find out why. If there was a problem, we needed to fix it right away. Spotting problems early gives you two advantages:

Spotting a problem early means you can solve it sooner. Those below-par numbers might be down for another week while we worked together to set things right, but they'd usually be back up in the fourth week. The entire cycle (problem identification – analysis – correction) took four weeks. That can't happen if you measure a KPI monthly.

If you measure every month, four weeks are gone before you see an indicator of a problem. Then you've only got that single data point, so it takes you more time to analyze and fix the problem. If you want to see if a pattern develops, two months are gone before you even begin to fix it. With a monthly measurement cycle, you have almost zero chance of fixing a problem so that it doesn't affect quarterly results.

There's another advantage to catching problems early: They're usually easier to solve. The longer a problem lives, the bigger and the nastier it gets. If your KPIs help you catch problems early, you improve the odds of a good outcome.

The "Key" in Key Performance Indicators means that you concentrate on the most important measures. Choose no more than five. Then give your choices my "Tropical Island Test."

Imagine that you're vacationing on a distant tropical island. It's lovely there, but it's very remote. Communications are severely limited. In fact, you can only receive a single five-line text message per week to let you know how things are going at the company.

You want to stay as long as possible because it's beautiful and peaceful, but you know that you have to head back if anything serious starts to go wrong. What things should you learn from your weekly text message?

You want the five items that sum up the state of the business for you. You don't have room for more, so you would select the five Performance Indicators that are truly Key.

That's your challenge right now. Identify the five Key Performance Indicators that will predict and drive the success of your current business model. That only took one sentence for me to write, but it may take you more than one work session to nail down.

Remember:

- Pick KPIs that drive and predict the financial results of your current business model.
- Pick KPIs that you can measure every week, where possible.
- Pick only the five (or fewer) KPIs that make the biggest difference.

Have you got your five KPIs? Great! The next thing you should do is set performance thresholds. Take a look at the hypothetical chart for fictional company B on the following page.

You want to make your decisions using something very much like this chart. You know what your KPIs are, but just knowing that the number of New Qualified Leads in the pipeline (for example) is important doesn't tell you enough. You must decide what the thresholds are for minimum acceptable performance and for solidly good performance. Start with the minimum acceptable level.

Figure 12: Key Performance Indicators – fictional company B

What Key Performance Indicators will predict and drive the future success of your current business model?

Key Performance Indicator	Red	Yellow	Green	Measurement Frequency	Person Accountable
New qualified leads	15		20	Weekly	Mila
Clients Sold	5		7	Weekly	Jonel
Average sale value	$4500		$5000	Weekly	Pierre
Employee % billable	80%		85%	Weekly	Laura
Customer service incidents	2		0	Monthly	Han

Source: Business Execution for RESULTS

The minimum acceptable level is the level of performance where you can keep the lights on but not much more. You're not making any progress at that level. In our example, that threshold for the number of New Qualified Leads in the pipeline is 15. Above that, you're OK, but just barely. Below that, you're in trouble. Put that number in the red column to indicate that it requires immediate attention.

Now set the threshold for solidly good performance. This is the level of performance you need to see delivered consistently if your company is making progress. For our example, the threshold is 20. That number goes in the green column to indicate that things are going well.

There's no need to put a number in the yellow column. Yellow indicates any level of performance above the minimum threshold, but not the level you really expect. Some companies like to put a range of numbers here, but others just leave it blank. This column is yellow to alert you that performance could be in the red unless you take action.

Now there's one more thing you should do. Assign one person to be accountable for performance on each KPI. Many people can be involved, but single-point accountability is essential.

The KPIs you've just identified will help you track the activities that are critical for success in your current business model, but they don't cover everything. Business Execution for RESULTS also requires that you make sure that you've got KPIs for every functional area of your company. That's what the next chapter is all about.

Organizational Structure and Role KPIs

So far we've talked about KPIs for your current business model. In this chapter, we'll shift our attention to what I call Role KPIs. I want to make sure that you have someone responsible for each of the functional areas in the business.

Role KPIs will be slightly different for every company. Most companies will have people in functional roles like marketing, sales, finance, operations, etc., but there will be differences from industry to industry. Walmart, Ritz-Carlton, and Toyota are all large, successful companies, but they have some different key roles because they are in different industries.

Walmart has always been a retail company, but the Walmart of today is very different from the Walmart of 1963. Back then, a guy named Sam Walton did all the buying and arranged for all the transportation. Today, there are different senior people responsible for logistics in the USA and elsewhere. There are individual senior managers responsible for procurement in individual business lines. Walmart in 1963 and Walmart today have different key roles because they're different-sized companies, in different stages of growth.

Amazon, Apple, and Walmart are all giant companies. They have all been successful, but they are very different. The key roles in those companies are different because their Value Disciplines are different.

No matter what industry it is in, what size it is, or what Value Discipline it practices, every company has three kinds of work that must get done: Every company has to acquire customers. Every company has to do things that deliver on its Value Discipline. And every company has support work, like accounting and HR.

- You will maximize growth and profits when:
- You have clear duties and KPIs for each functional role.
- You have the right people in each role.
- Those people concentrate on the right things.
- They are held accountable for performance every month.

Your first task is to determine what the functional roles are. I'm not talking about your organizational chart, that diagram that indicates who reports to whom and who everyone's boss is. You might have marketing and sales as key functional roles, even though your organization chart shows the sales manager reporting to the marketing director.

When I work with companies, we develop a chart with the following columns:

- Role: what needs to be done
- Person accountable for it
- KPI: the specific KPI measurement for each role
- The KPI score (target threshold) that indicates acceptable performance

Take a look at the chart on the following page to get an idea of what a hypothetical, filled-in chart might look like for fictional company C.

Identifying the roles is crucial. It's natural for you to think of this as either the person in the role now or as the title that a person holds, but you need to forget about people for now and just start by listing the key functional roles that need to be performed.

You should have at least one each for acquiring customers, implementing your Value Discipline, and supporting the business. Some roles may not be full-time jobs yet. In other words, if you're a small to mid-sized company, you will often have a single person responsible for several roles. That will change as you grow.

If you're a start-up, the founders probably split up the important roles among themselves. The company will add people as it grows, depending on need. Here's how things went for one startup:

Tom and two partners founded a business to sell niche software solutions to large corporations. Tom was responsible for sales and marketing. Another partner was the entire engineering department, responsible for creating the actual products. The third partner filled all the administrative roles. He took care of accounting and finance and all the other record keeping.

It took three years for them to gain traction while funding the company with their credit cards and second mortgages on their homes. They hired a programmer as their first employee.

Figure 13: Functional role KPI's – fictional company C

Functional Role	Person Accountable	KPI	Role KPI Target: The required level of performance that will be assessed MONTHLY		
			Red	Yellow	Green
Head of Company	Fred	Net profit %	<10%		>20%
Head of Marketing	Mary	New Qualified leads / month	<150		>200
	Mary	Cost of Client Acquisition (COCA)	>$4000		<$3000
Head of Sales	Peter	Lead / Sales conversion %	<20%		>30%
	Peter	Monthly Recurring Revenue (MRR)	$450		$500
Head of Operations	Raoul	Client Lifetime Value (LTV)	<15 mths		>18 mths
	Raoul	Client Monthly Churn	>5%		<3%
Head of Finance	Lupe	Accounts receivable days	>35 days		<25 days
Head of HR	Lisa	Employee turnover	3%		1%
Head of Customer Satisfaction	Susan	Client Net Promoter Score	NPS <30%		NPS >50%
Head of Business Unit (A)	Vadim	Unit (A) Net Profit %	<5%		>10%
Head of Business Unit (B)	Ming	Unit (B) Net Profit %	<20%		>30%
Sales representative/s	(Various)	Number of Clients sold /month	10		14

Source: Business Execution for RESULTS

At that point, they decided that they really needed to have titles. Tom became the CEO. He was now the one with profit and loss responsibility, but he was still responsible for all the sales and marketing. The engineering partner became the Vice President for Product Management, and the administrative partner took the title of VP of Administration.

The titles were fanciful, but also inspirational. Tom remembers that they also listed their address on business cards under the words "World Headquarters." In time they added people and grew into the titles. The company added a marketing director, but Tom, with his CEO title, was responsible for both overall company performance and sales for quite a while.

When companies grow, they add levels and role specialists. Here's how Rich Mironov described the process in his book, *The Art of Product Management: Lessons from a Silicon Valley Innovator*:

> One rule of thumb is that organizations have to add a new layer of management each time they triple their total staff. A company of ten needs a CEO. A company of 30 also needs VPs. At 90, expect to see Directors as well as VPs.

You know that things will change as you grow. For now, though, list the key functional roles and the person currently responsible for each one. Effective performance in these key roles is crucial to your business model success, regardless of who the incumbents in those roles are.

Now add the Key Performance Indicator for each role. One KPI per role is ideal. Two is the maximum. A KPI for the marketing function might be new sales leads or proposals submitted per month. KPIs for the finance function might be Days Sales Outstanding or Free Cash.

Your Value Discipline will influence your choice of which functional roles and their associated performance indicators are crucial for your firm. Southwest Airlines practices the Operational Excellence Value Discipline. One of their key functional KPIs is the average time it takes to "turn" a flight. That's measured from the arrival of a plane at the gate until the time that same plane pulls back for its next flight.

Procter and Gamble practices Product Leadership. One of their key functional KPIs is the percentage of new products that meet their revenue and profit targets. Another key measure is the percentage of new products that have a component developed outside P&G.

One of the legendary firms in Customer Intimacy is Ritz-Carlton. They compete in the luxury hotel industry where the average turnover for front-line employees is 158 percent per year. Ritz-Carlton wants to keep turnover below 18 percent, but also higher than 15 percent, because "fresh voices are valuable, too."

Just as you did with your overall company (business model) KPIs, you need to add actual performance thresholds for each Role KPI. Follow the procedure we outlined in the last chapter. Begin with the minimum threshold, the level to keep the lights on but nothing more. Then add your green measure, the solid level of performance you expect consistently. Your yellow level is between those two thresholds. Note the specific range if it helps you.

Most of the companies I work with start with a list of Role KPIs that needs to be tweaked to make it more effective. That's what we're going to do next.

Do you have any roles where more than one person is accountable for results? If you do, you need to assign the role to one person. Single-point accountability is absolutely critical if you want continued success. Two people can't be accountable for the same role. One person must take responsibility. If you have two business owners, only one of you can be CEO. You can't all be accountable for marketing, either. The rule is one person per role.

Now consider the people you have assigned to each role. Does the role play to their natural strengths? Do they have the knowledge, skills, and abilities to do the job effectively? One way that several companies have analyzed this is to ask, "If we were hiring someone to fulfill this role, would we re-hire this person?" If not, someone else needs to become the one accountable for the role.

Do you have any unassigned roles? If you do, how will you fill them?

Do you have any people who are fulfilling multiple roles? Can they do justice to all their responsibilities? If not, you need to make other arrangements.

Look at your answers to the questions above. Now make a list of organizational changes you need to make, set a due date, and assign one person the responsibility for making each change.

There's one more thing before we go on: You should measure your performance on Role KPIs every month and hold your assigned person accountable for results. As with so many other things, Peter Drucker said it well:

> Leaders owe it to the organization and their fellow workers not to tolerate non-performing people in important jobs.

Accountability is meaningless without consequences. Sometimes we need to make an example of poor performance. Sometimes we even need to let someone go.

You can be fairly sure of one thing: Your team probably already knows who the poor performers are. They're just waiting to see whether or not you're going to do anything about it, whether or not you're serious about accountability for performance.

Are your people in each functional role being held accountable every month for achieving the performance they're responsible for? Are there positive consequences if they do well? What are the negative consequences if they don't?

Now you've got things covered. You have Company KPIs for your current business model and Role KPI's for each of the key functional roles in your business. How do you stay on top of it all to ensure Business Execution for RESULTS? That's what our next chapter, "Performance Made Visible," is about.

Performance Made Visible

Why do so many great plans come to nothing?

As I noted at the beginning of this book, experts tell us that between 60 percent and 90 percent of all strategic initiatives fail to achieve their objectives. Our own experience working with companies bears this out.

At one point in its history, RESULTS.com earned fees primarily by helping clients to develop effective strategic plans, plans that improved the odds of success. We would work with clients for two days at the beginning of the year, using the disciplined process you've been experiencing to create a well-thought-through strategic plan.

Then we'd return every quarter to review progress and update their plans. We'd help them perform an updated reality check (SWOT analysis) and align their plan with the new reality. Then we'd help them choose their new Strategic Projects and Numerical Targets for the next quarter.

We would all feel great at the end of the quarterly sessions. The business leaders and their teams would tell us how aligned and focused and motivated they felt. They knew what their new projects and targets were. They were ready to charge off again on another 90-day sprint.

Unfortunately, when we got together again after three months had elapsed, we would ask them whether they had completed their Strategic Projects, and they would shuffle and look down at their feet. We would ask to see how their KPIs had been tracking. More shuffling. Then the excuses would come out:

We got too busy and just could not get it done.
We were too optimistic in our goal setting.
We got distracted by another opportunity and focused
on that instead.
We forgot to measure our KPIs and keep them updated.

Our clients are very smart people. They had robust strategic plans that were updated every quarter to address the current reality. But they weren't getting the results they wanted.

What was happening to them was something that happens to almost everyone. It happens to me, and it will happen to you if you let it. We let the urgent drive out the important. We put off doing things, believing we can catch up later. We let ourselves think that we're doing OK, but we don't ever compare that gut feeling to real data. You have to find a way of linking strategic planning to business execution.

We decided that, if we were going to provide consulting services to a client, they had to agree to meet with us for a one-hour virtual meeting each week to check on progress and to agree on the key action items that needed to get done in the coming week to move their Strategic Projects and KPIs forward. We called these "weekly execution meetings," and they made a world of difference in terms of getting the right things done.

Now clients were being held accountable by an external third party every week for tracking and driving their KPIs, and for implementing their Strategic Projects on time. We got very good at running these meetings to drive execution. We also taught our clients key success habits and helped them to implement these practices to make their companies even more effective at business execution. The weekly consulting sessions became a core service offering. RESULTS.com became "the business execution experts."

We made sure that our clients kept the important things "top of mind" and that they took meaningful action on their Strategic Projects and KPIs every week. We kept our clients on a short leash, helped them avoid distractions, and made sure they stayed focused on their stated goals.

Interestingly, we have found that when working with a client firm, after about 12 to 18 months, we have taught them everything we know. We have covered all the things you have read about in this book, and we have worked with the business leaders and their teams to teach them execution disciplines and how to make those part of the DNA of their firm. By this stage, the business is very good at setting and executing strategy.

But many of them continue to engage with a consultant on a weekly basis long after we've taught them everything we had to teach. They like having an external third party challenging them every step of the way and keeping them on track. They like the discipline that we impose. They like the tough questions we ask.

Even though the weekly execution meetings dramatically improved our clients' performance against goals, we knew they could do better. We developed simple tracking methods that our clients could use to track their own performance between meetings.

In the beginning, those were manual systems like electronic whiteboards and Excel spreadsheets, and we tried all kinds of methods to see if we could find something that would make performance visible – if people can see how they're doing on the important things, they're more likely to attend to those important things. And if their performance is visible to their peers, we've found that it acts as a spur to improved performance. The Navy could have told us that.

One of the most difficult and demanding tasks in aviation is landing on an aircraft carrier. People who've learned to fly will tell you that landing an airplane is hard all by itself. Now think about landing on a small field that's moving forward while pitching and rolling. Bad weather and equipment problems can make it even harder.

Every carrier landing is graded for safety and technique. Average scores are computed for every carrier pilot. Those average scores are posted where all the pilots can see them, ranked in order from best to worst. As a friend of mine told me, "No one wants to be on the bottom of that list."

Making performance visible has two advantages that come straight from human nature. When people are reminded of what's important and of how they're doing, they're more likely to do the important things. When they know that their performance is visible to others, they're more likely to push for excellence. People don't want to be "on the bottom of the board," and they don't want to let their colleagues down. Making individual performance visible also ties in with our principle of single-point accountability.

We learned that the level of performance should be visible at a glance. The way to make that happen is by having a quick color code for results. We recommend the standard red, yellow, and green of the traffic light. Results that are colored red are not up to standard; sound the alarm! Yellow is the minimum acceptable threshold that enables you to keep operating, and green is the target level of performance that you expect to be achieved most of the time, if the overall company is performing well and if people are performing well in their key functional roles.

We used to call our tracking system "dashboarding." Dashboards make performance visible. In your car, the dashboard tells you – at a glance – how fast you're going, how much fuel you have in the tank, and the status of basic systems like lubrication and engine cooling. If something starts to go wrong, your car sounds the alarm to let you know.

Our manual systems worked, but they had to be updated frequently, often by hand. That introduced the chance of error and the ever-present possibility that the dashboard didn't reflect the current reality. Also, the fact is that many people don't use spreadsheets, and those who do may not look at them every day. Software seemed like a solution to the manual updating problems.

Software-based business dashboards started appearing in the late 1990s. The first ones reflected the computerized reports of the pre-networked era. They showed traditional measures like sales and inventory turns, but not much more. Balanced scorecards added other measures, but early scorecards of all types were updated on the old manual schedules and not in real time. That changed for big companies first.

Some large firms, like General Electric, developed their own dashboard systems. Most bought enterprise systems built on databases by SAP and Oracle that incorporated dashboards. Those were great for big companies, but they were too expensive and complex for the companies we work with.

We reviewed software dashboarding programs as they were introduced. None of them did what we wanted. Many didn't address business execution issues. Some were great at financial and operational measures, but they didn't help much with goals and projects. Other programs were variations on project management. They tracked progress on goals, but they didn't have a link to the strategic plan.

A third group of software products claimed to help with business execution. But most of them had simply bolted a "business execution" module to a program designed for something else, usually an HR function such as performance appraisals and employee development. Using them was a little like driving in screws with a hammer: They got the job done, but with a lot of effort and a messy outcome.

We couldn't find anything that would do what we knew was important for business execution software. So we said, "The hell with it. Let's develop our own software." Here is the initial wish list of requirements we came up with:

- Offers a shared platform to view the Strategic Projects and Key Performance Indicators, so that everyone in the company knows what the strategic plan is and the important things they need to focus on to play their part
- Provides a helicopter view of how everyone is performing, including the ability to monitor team and individual progress at a glance
- Uses color coding to show whether a Strategic Project or KPI is on track
- Has the ability to assign tasks to specific individuals to move goals forward
- Displays daily reminders to hold people accountable and to make sure tasks are completed on time
- Runs more effective team and one-on-one meetings that drive the business forward
- Records meeting minutes and decisions made
- Enables real-time collaboration to capture conversations, discussions, and feedback
- Integrates with other commonly used business software
- Is available anywhere, anytime, on any device

I recommend using this checklist as a starting point for any system you choose or develop.

The growing demand for this type of solution is why RESULTS.com made the strategic decision to evolve our business from being a consulting firm that used software to support our consulting, to becoming a software firm that uses consulting to support our software. The execution of this strategy will no doubt change as the environment changes, and it will result in new opportunities that cannot be imagined yet, but I do know that making performance visible is vital to Business Execution for RESULTS!

Everything we've discussed so far in this book – in fact, everything about your strategy – comes together when you make performance visible. Before we move on to other ways of assuring that you continue to make progress and achieve your BHAG, we need to review some main points about how the numbers drive performance.

There are three kinds of numbers that you use to keep performance on track and drive achievement:

First, you should have Numerical Targets (outcome goals) that you display to everyone. They should help people understand what the company intends to achieve by the end of the quarter, by the end of year one, the end of year two, etc. These numbers are aligned to your budgets and forecasts and paint a picture of where the company is going and how what people do fits into the big picture.

Second, you need Company Key Performance Indicators (KPIs) that track and drive the success of your current business model. They should be truly "key." You should identify a handful of leading indicators, so that, if these numbers exceed the desired performance threshold on a weekly basis, it will ultimately be reflected in the results on your financial statements at the end of the month. Remember: financial results are lagging indicators.

Third, you need Functional Role KPIs that measure how effectively the key functional roles (and the people responsible for them) are performing.

You also need to check the execution progress of your Strategic Projects. Are they on track?

You should have performance thresholds for every KPI and color-code performance in red, yellow, or green. That will help you identify trouble spots, danger zones, and on-target performance.

It's important to set your goals and performance targets so that they help you achieve long-term success. Here's where I see many firms come unstuck.

Most entrepreneurs and high-performing team members are optimists by nature. They like to set themselves challenging goals and targets, and they're sure that everything will turn out well.

Unfortunately, what I often see happen is that they set their Numerical Targets and the green performance thresholds for their KPIs so high that they seldom reach them. They justify that by saying, "Aim for the stars and you might reach the moon." In other words, even if you miss the really high goal, you'll still do very, very well.

That might work for some people, but it doesn't work for most of us. It has the effect of showing people always being "in the red" in term of how their performance is displayed. The proof is on their dashboard every day. They get used to being in the red. After a while it becomes the norm. They can become apathetic: "What's the use?" Also, if they do not feel like they can immediately turn the score around, being in the red starts to become the norm – and people decide that if being in the red is always the case, then being in the red must be OK. A culture of mediocrity develops.

Remember the SMART acronym that we discussed in the chapter titled "What Should We Do Now?": The A in a SMART goal stands for Achievable. That works in accord with our human nature. Recently, there's been scientific proof to back this up.

Researchers Teresa Amabile and Steven Kramer looked at 12,000 daily work-diary entries from more than two hundred people, and they identified what they call the "progress principle." People love to make progress, and even minor progress events can be powerful motivators. I like to call those events "small wins."

Small wins are the incremental steps toward our longer term goals. The research showed that when people can see tangible progress and experience "small wins" often, they become more engaged and productive.

That's where business execution software (dashboarding software) can be so powerful. These tools let your people see progress on their goals and KPIs every step of the way. It's better to set Relevant and Achievable goals, get your people used to "winning," and then ratchet up the performance threshold over time.

The same principle applied when I was bodybuilding – especially during my bulking-up phase. I used the concept of KPIs and applied it diligently in my training. I recorded the exercises I did, how much weight I used, and how many reps and sets I achieved.

I might have a goal (Numerical Target) of doing sets of bench presses with 400 pounds (180kg) on the bar by the end of the year. But if I'm currently only bench-pressing 350 pounds, then putting 400 pounds on the bar today and expecting to be able to lift it is both dangerous and stupid. Instead, I need to add a couple of extra pounds to the bar and work my way up to 400 pounds over time, something like the following:

I set my "green" level of performance as bench-pressing 355 pounds this month. During the month I'll get used to doing reps with that weight, and I'll feel good about the progress I make. I'm working hard and "in the green" with my training for the whole month. Next month, I might raise my green level of KPI performance to 360 pounds. Now, in order to achieve my training KPI for bench presses, I need to be doing sets and reps with 360 pounds. The month after that I could raise the green level to 365 pounds.

I still need to train as hard as I can and make performance visible so I don't kid myself into thinking I'm working hard and making progress. I also need to make as much progress as possible, and that means setting aggressive goals. But I need to recalibrate my green performance threshold every month so that the weight I'm using and the reps I'm doing are Relevant and Achievable based on where I am in my training cycle. Sometimes that means lowering my monthly goal.

There's a cycle to bodybuilding competition: You bulk up and get bigger and stronger for months, but then you have to start dieting to be ready for a competition. I had to follow a strict food discipline so that every bit of fat melted away to show my new, more muscular body underneath. That created another goal-setting challenge.

You see, your body weight has a direct correlation with how much weight you can lift, so, as my body weight plummeted, I had to adjust my lifting goals downward. In the bodybuilding pre-contest phase, lifting a weight that I could handle easily only a month or so before would quickly become impossible. When I was dieting, my exercise goals and green level of performance needed to be adjusted downward so they were Achievable and Relevant to the situation.

Every business I've ever seen has some kind of cycle to contend with. You must keep your goals Achievable and Relevant when you're in the upward part of the cycle. Small wins along the way add up to big wins. But when you're in a downward part of the cycle, you must adjust your goals to match the reality of the situation.

So set reasonable targets and decide how often to measure them. Assign a single person to be accountable for achieving every performance target.

Once you've defined your KPIs and the person accountable for each one, you should track performance so you can spot potential problems early. There was a time when you had to do that manually, but now software can make tracking easier and more effective.

The numbers, and how you track them, are important, but they're only measures. Your people create the performance that the numbers measure. So if you want the numbers to come out right, you need to do the right things with your human capital. That's what we'll turn to in the next section.

Getting the Most from Human Capital

Introduction

Jack Welch was *Fortune* magazine's "Manager of the Century." Welch worked at General Electric for forty years and was the CEO for twenty of them. During his tenure as CEO, GE's market capitalization soared from $13 billion to $400 billion. Welch thought that hiring, evaluating, and developing people was the most important thing he did when he was CEO. In his book, *Winning*, he summed up why:

> Nothing matters more in winning than getting the right people on the field. All the clever strategies and advanced technologies in the world are nowhere near as effective without great people to put them to work.

If you need more convincing, here's a quote from Peter Drucker:

> The ability to make good decisions regarding people represents one of the last reliable sources of competitive advantage, since very few organizations are very good at it.

That's what this section is all about: getting the most from your human capital. In today's knowledge economy, people, with their knowledge and relationships, are the only source of sustainable competitive advantage. It's people who turn your strategy into results. That's why people should be treated as assets, not costs.

Costs should be controlled and limited and even eliminated. But you want assets to grow. You cut costs, but you invest in assets.

Business Execution for RESULTS begins with hiring A-Players. Before you begin the actual hiring, you need to be clear about your values. I introduced the concept of Core Values earlier when we were working on your BHAG.

Your Core Values are nothing more than what you expect from people. Your A-Players are people with the right knowledge, skills, and abilities whose Core Values match up with your Core Values. You certainly want talented people, but you want those people to fit your Core Values, or you're headed for trouble down the road.

You'll go through some exercises that will help you clearly specify and articulate your Core Value statements and then move to the process of hiring. The companies that do the best job of hiring have three things in common: They have clear performance standards so they know exactly what they're looking for. They have a rigorous hiring process that will increase the odds that they've made the right choice. And they are ruthlessly disciplined about using that process every time they hire.

Hiring people is just the beginning of getting the most from your human capital. The people you hire will show up on the first day of work, ready to go. They're motivated, and you want to keep them that way. You'll learn how to do that in the chapter on "Onboarding and Developing People."

Big companies have elaborate onboarding processes. You won't need anything like that. You will need a simple process that harnesses the energy and enthusiasm that your new hire shows up with. And, of course, you need the discipline to carry it out.

Great companies also help people develop. They invest in the person's future. This is one of those win-win activities. People naturally want to make progress, so they perceive development opportunities as a benefit. And you want the people you hire to grow and become more accomplished and increase their asset value the longer they stay with the company.

This is one place where you can learn from the big companies. When you strip away all the departments and courses and assessments, the great people-development companies do the same thing: They have a process where performance review and discussion of what's next are a regular part of the cadence of the business. I'll show you how to do that in your company.

All the people things in this section set the stage for the words that are on everyone's lips these days: employee engagement. The "Engaging People at Work" chapter is one of the most significant in this book. Engagement is important because companies with higher levels of employee engagement grow faster and make more money than the competition. The foundation of engagement is your Core Purpose.

Your Core Purpose is what your people work for that's beyond the numbers we use to measure things in business. It's what makes work meaningful. You'll answer a series of questions that will help you define your Core Purpose so you can express it in a simple, concise statement. Then you can move on to the things you can do that will drive engagement.

There's a lot of hype and nonsense out there about employee engagement. I'll cut through all that for you and bring the issue down to the things that you and your team leaders can do that will increase engagement. Then, I'll wrap up the chapter and the section by showing you a simple way you can measure it.

When you're ready, turn the page, and we'll start you on the road to getting the most from human capital.

Defining Your Core Values

Southwest Airlines is the most profitable airline in the history of the USA. The company was founded in 1971; 1973 was its first full year of profitability, and Southwest has been profitable every year since then. That's 39 consecutive years as I write this. Other airlines have come and gone. No other airline has matched Southwest's record.

There's no one secret to success like that, but one key to Southwest's success is its culture, "the way we do things around here." One of Southwest's most powerful cultural values is related to the concept of "fun."

You know about fun if you've ever taken a Southwest flight. My experience is probably typical: I've heard Southwest flight attendants sing the safety instructions; I've seen them in costumes; I've heard them ad lib little bits to liven up the standard safety language. No other airline seems to have fun like Southwest.

That's no accident. Southwest is clear about its values, and it hires people who have the same values and will fit into the culture. That's simple, but not easy.

Southwest's number-one hiring criterion, the one they look for first, is a sense of humor. People with the right skills and a sense of humor are A-Players for Southwest. In some ways, their hiring process is like that of every other company that hires well. They have a clear idea of what knowledge, skills, and abilities they're looking for. They check references. But there's more.

Southwest has designed a hiring process that helps them make smart decisions about whether a candidate has a sense of humor. Candidates are interviewed by groups of Southwest employees. The process is longer than most, but, in the end, Southwest Airlines winds up with people who fit.

That's where you want to wind up, too. Business Execution for RESULTS requires you to be clear about your Core Values so you can make them part of your hiring criteria. You'll need to design a rigorous hiring process and follow it every time. That's not easy, but it's how great companies hire the A-Players who drive their success. So let's start by looking at your Core Values.

Here's a reminder of what your Core Values do for your company, besides guide your hiring. I've already introduced them to you in the first part of the book.

Your Core Values provide a moral compass for your people. They can help people decide on the right course, regardless of the challenge they face.

Your Core Values give you a basis for consistent decision making by everyone. When people share the same Core Values, they tend to make decisions in the same way.

Get your team together. Let's try to clarify what your Core Values are right now. Here are two ways that other companies have used to define their Core Values:

First, think about starting your company from scratch: Which five people would you rehire because they behave the way you expect your people to behave? Forget functional skills and roles for a moment and identify people who act the way you want everyone in your company to act, regardless of role.

Identify the behaviors that are common to all these people. Describe those behaviors in short, concise, three- to five-word descriptive statements. What did you come up with?

Here's another way to get at your values: What behaviors has your company always been known for or stood for, no matter what the circumstances? If you want to really develop this line of thought, contact some of your customers and ask them what you're known for. Put the answers into three- to five-word descriptive statements.

Let's see if we can make some decisions. What are the top five behaviors that you want demonstrated by everyone in your company? State each one in three to five words like James Wren & Company did with their Core Value I described earlier in the book: "Three coats means three coats."

Consider your Value Discipline when you're crafting your Core Values. If Operational Excellence is your discipline, one of your values should probably reflect efficiency and cost control. If you chose Product Leadership, one of your Core Values should probably include something on innovation. And, if you picked Customer Intimacy, one of your Core Values should probably emphasize how you work with customers.

I asked you to do five because that works well when I do this with clients in person. There's no rule that you should have exactly five values. Zappos has more, but my view is that your people should know them by heart, so it needs to be a manageable and memorable list.

I recommend using three- to five-word statements, because one-word values statements are too ambiguous and not very helpful. In three to five words, you should be able to state very clearly the type of behavior you expect from your people.

My view is that having Core Values like "honesty and integrity" is a waste of time. These are table-stakes behaviors for any company and are not things that are unique to your firm and your culture. You are not going to hire or keep anyone who is dishonest and a liar, are you?

Your Core Values are "musts." They are not just "nice-to-haves." Use the following questions to test whether the values you've listed are really "core":

- Would you confront a colleague if he or she were not demonstrating this value?
- Would you spend money or leave money on the table to uphold this value?
- Would you fire someone for violating this value, even if he or she were an excellent performer otherwise?

Your Core Values must pass all three tests.

Once you've created your list of Core Values, you need to make sure that they're visible and that people remember them so that they can act on them. Some companies have found creative ways to help people remember their Core Values.

AnswerLab defined seven Core Values for their firm. Here they are:

Build trust
Provide amazing service
Jump in to help others

Handle change with flexibility
Innovate our processes
Figure it out and get it done
Make AnswerLab a great place to work

Those are great, but they're hard to remember. You can do the usual things that companies do to keep their values visible. You can put them on plaques that you post around the office and on little cards that everyone carries in their pocket. You can even recite them every day. AnswerLab did something creative. They created a mnemonic device to help people remember. It's a simple sentence:

Beer Pong Judges Have Incredible Floor Mops

They also illustrate the mnemonic device with a picture of – well, I'll leave it to your imagination, but you can bet it helps their people remember the Core Values.

Remembering is just the beginning. You should make your Core Values an explicit part of the way you do business. Reference them when you make management decisions. At every weekly meeting, share stories of people in the company who have done a great job of exemplifying one of the Core Values. You may even give a monthly award to the person who best exemplified the Core Values.

Your Core Values determine the way you do everything that involves people at your company. Talk about your Core Values every day in the normal course of business to help drive engagement. Make them a key part of your performance appraisal process. We'll talk about those things a little further along in this book.

Now we're going to turn to recruiting: how you go about hiring A-Players.

Hiring A-Players

I currently live in Los Angeles, where John Wooden forged his legacy as one of the best coaches of any kind, ever. Wooden's UCLA teams won ten NCAA Men's Basketball Championships. The next closest coaches have won four each.

Wooden's UCLA teams had four perfect, 30-win seasons. At one point, they had won 88 straight games. In fact, in a 40-year coaching career from high school to college, Wooden's teams had only one losing season. That's simply incredible.

John Wooden is also known for his wise sayings. Here's one of them:

> The team with the best players wins.

That's true, but you have to consider the whole sentence. Most businesses act like they believe that there's a kind of generic great player out there who will fit into any system. That's not so.

Harvard professor Boris Groysberg studied the idea that a great player would be a great player anywhere. Then he wrote a book titled *Chasing Stars: The Myth of Talent and the Portability of Performance.* His research reminds us that we have to pay attention to the whole quote if we're going to take John Wooden's advice. Let me re-state it. The italics are mine.

> The *team* with the best players wins.

Business Execution for RESULTS requires you have the right people for your team. Hiring those A-Players begins with setting standards.

You want people with the same Core Values. You want people who will perform superbly in the roles you have. Those are the A-Players who are right for your team.

Your Core Values set the behavioral standard for the kind of people you want to hire. These essential behaviors ("how we do things around here") are the same for every person and every role in your company.

Each of those roles also has performance standards. We use a Role Score-card form to outline standards for every role in a client company. Role

Scorecards should be reviewed quarterly and updated as needed. Roles will change over time, especially if your company is growing rapidly.

These Role Scorecards change slightly from time to time and company to company, but they should include something like the following elements. Add or remove elements as needed.

What is the **Functional Role?** This is the role (what needs to be done), not the title or the person filling the role at the moment. You may find it helpful to review the chapter on "Organizational Structure and Role KPIs."

What are the **Reporting Relationships?** What role (not person) does this role report to? What roles report to this one? This is a good time to review the span of control for each role and determine if it has too many direct reports to be effective.

What is the **Purpose of the Role?** Use my Twitter rule to create a single short sentence to describe the purpose in plain language. Avoid jargon.

What **Key Duties & Outcomes** are expected? This is a list of the critical tasks that the person in the role needs to perform and the results they need to achieve for each task in order to be successful. List them in descending order of importance so people know what actions and results they need to prioritize. Take a close look at this every quarter, because this is where roles will change.

Listing and prioritizing force you to think through which tasks are really important for successful performance in this role. Be very specific. There should be no excuses for employees not knowing exactly what outcomes and duties are expected of them and where they should be spending most of their time.

List your **Core Values** on every Role Scorecard as a reminder that demonstrating these behaviors is a key component of successful performance.

Every role should have at least one **Key Performance Indicator** that defines the performance you expect every month. We discussed how to set the level of performance represented by the green, yellow, and red color codes in the chapter, "Performance Made Visible."

What follows are the elements of the Scorecard you need to add for hiring purposes:

What are the key **Behavioral Competencies** that the person in this role needs to demonstrate in order to be successful? Here's a list I choose from:

- Intelligence
- Analysis / Problem solving
- Decision making
- Creativity
- Strategic thinking
- Risk taking
- Leading edge thinking
- Experience in a similar role
- Integrity
- Resourcefulness / Initiative
- Time management
- Independence
- Stress management
- Self-awareness
- Adaptability
- Customer focus
- Team player
- Assertiveness / Persuasion
- Presentation skills
- Negotiation skills
- Energy
- Leadership (*"Outward focus"* = *visionary; can rally the whole team to a better future*)
- Management (*"Inward focus"* = *coaching; works one-on-one with staff to maximize individual performance*)

Note the distinction between leadership and management. I picked this up from Marcus Buckingham, and I've found that it works very well. One competency is not better than the other. Many unhelpful books have made it seem like leadership is good, management is bad. Both competencies are important for business success. Some people are good at leadership. Some people are good at management. A rare few are good at both. Some people aren't cut out for either, and that's OK, too.

For each role, pick the ten most important and rank them in descending order of importance. Then narrow it down to the top five. The top five on your list must be the absolutely crucial behavioral competencies someone would need to possess in order to have a chance of getting hired and succeeding in the role.

Next, consider the **Qualifications** you want to establish for this role. Qualifications are things like degrees, certifications, and licenses. List them as either "must-haves" or "nice-to-haves."

Licenses will almost always be must-haves since they're necessary for the person to perform the duties of the role. I suggest using actual skills tests on those with technical certificates, since a certificate alone may not be proof of the competency you require. Finally, I've found that formal education becomes less and less relevant as a qualification the longer a person has been in the workforce.

Skills and Experience: Skills should be specific for each role. For both skills and experience, indicate what is a must-have and what's a nice-to-have.

No matter what you list in the last three categories, you should consider them minimums. They're table stakes. A-Players go beyond these and continue to grow and develop their skills. This is a good time to define what we mean by "A-Players."

- A-Players are people who *consistently* exceed the target level of performance for their role. Their KPIs are unfailingly in the green. In many cases, they raise the targets for their role over time.
- A-Players are people who *consistently* demonstrate behaviors that match your Core Values. In many cases, they become role models of your Core Values whom others use as an example.

Those two criteria are not negotiable. If you intend to create a great company, you need to fill it with top performers who live your Core Values every day. Hiring people who can do that calls for a rigorous process that you use every time you hire.

As we developed and improved our process at RESULTS.com, we imagined ourselves as curators of excellent business practices. We identified the most effective practices, the ones that get great results for many different kinds of companies. Then we adapted those practices so that they fit into a coherent system which I describe in this book, Business Execution for RESULTS. That's precisely what we did with the hiring practices called "Topgrading."

Topgrading was developed by psychologist Brad Smart, and it grew from three insights. While in college and graduate school, Brad worked in HR departments and noticed how often companies hired the wrong people, thereby increasing costs and decreasing productivity. His PhD studies concentrated on hiring processes, and he learned that there simply wasn't much material on hiring top performers. After getting his doctorate, Brad joined a firm of psychologists where he discerned that, even with the most sophisticated screening techniques, most hires were not the top performers that everyone wanted.

The Topgrading process will require you to put in a lot of time and effort. At some point, you're almost sure to ask whether that extra work pays off. Rather than wait, I'm going to address that concern now, beginning with why hiring A-Players pays off.

Top performers beat their lower performing peers by multiples, not just a few percentage points. McKinsey & Company research indicates that A-Players outperform average workers by as much as 250 percent.

Bad hires are expensive: The average cost to replace a person is five to 15 times their base salary. That's a lot of money. And it doesn't count the cost of disruption or the extra work that people have to do while the position is vacant.

A-Players like to work with other A-Players. The more A-Players you have on your team, the less likely it is that other A-Players will leave, thereby lowering your turnover.

Those are the reasons why you want to have as many A-Players on your team as possible. But why should you put in the effort I'm going to suggest? That answer is simple.

Less rigorous processes simply don't work as well. The typical hiring process results in hiring an A-Player only about one out of four times, or 25 percent. Using the rigorous method you're about to learn, you can increase that to 70 to 90 percent.

Here's a simple rule to remember: Hire slow and fire fast. Unfortunately, most companies do it the other way; they hire fast and take a long time to fire someone who can't or won't perform.

I know you're in a hurry. It's natural to feel that the most important thing is to get that open position filled. Resist that temptation. Your objective is to put an A-Player in that role, someone who will be a top performer for a long time.

That's the goal: If possible, you want to hire A-Players for every role. To make that happen, you need standards and a process. You've already set the standards for the role with the Role Scorecard.

You've probably noticed that the Role Scorecard I have described is a far more focused and specific document than a typical job description, but you should be able to capture it all on one page. Don't just use it in the hiring process – everyone should keep their Role Scorecard in sight at their desk or workstation and review it regularly.

You're going to advertise the role and, if you're a great company, you should attract great applicants. But you can't depend on people out there to know you're great, so you need to market yourself as an employer.

You need to market your company to employees with the same vigor that you use to market to your customers. You need to clearly spell out who you are: your Core Values, your Core Purpose, your BHAG, your Strategic Position, and your Brand Promise.

Use the Role Scorecard as the basis for your advertisement, so people know exactly what they're in for. You want to use your time effectively, and doing the advertisement this way helps. You don't want hundreds of people applying; you just want the right people applying. That's what will happen with the kind of job ad I've described. A-Players will say, "Oh, yes, that's for me!" Most B and C players will deselect themselves from even applying.

Send everyone who applies a Career History Form. Applicants will typically send you a résumé, because they think you want to see it. Ignore it. Résumés are sales documents that present selective bits of information in the most favorable way. They will not help you hire A-Players, but the Career History Form will.

Everyone needs to fill out a Career History Form if they want to apply for a role. If they don't fill it out, they don't get an interview. You only want people who are really interested in your position.

A Career History Form is a detailed life / work history. It should gather information about a candidate's education and experience. Ask about specific duties, specific achievements, and successes and failures. You're not just looking for the details of education and work experience here. You're also looking for self-awareness and the willingness to do the work of filling out the form. Here are some things I recommend you ask for on your Career History Form:

- Educational grades
- Employment for every year and month since they began working
- Compensation – starting and ending salary for each role
- Results and achievements for each role – quantified with numbers
- Failures or mistakes experienced – and what they learned from them
- What they liked most and least about each role
- Name and title of supervisor in each role
- What each supervisor would indicate they were good at / not good at
- Permission to speak to each of their previous managers

A Career History Form should require time and effort to complete. It is the second line of screening. People with a sketchy work history or who really don't fit the role you're hiring for or who are used to explaining away their less-than-stellar performance will opt out of the process by not completing the form.

By requiring a very detailed Career History Form, you screen in only those people who are proud of their history and willing to share details of it. This is the first place in the process where you're likely to notice that A-Players are different from the others.

Use the completed Career History Forms to decide who you want to interview. Notify any applicants who didn't make the cut right away. Don't leave people in limbo.

Conduct the interviews according to principles that come straight from the Topgrading book. Dr. Smart uses the acronym CIDS for interview format. Those letters stand for Chronological, In-Depth, and Structured. The principles apply to both phone interviews and the ones you conduct in person.

Chronological means that you consider the events in the candidate's life in order. That makes it easier to spot patterns of behavior. It makes it more likely that you'll discover how a candidate has grown from his or her first job until now. And it helps make sure that you don't miss anything.

In-Depth means that you have to dig for details. Past behavior is the best indicator of future behavior, so you want to find out everything you can about what the applicant did in the past. You want to turn up detailed specifics. A-Players will usually give them to you. Others will decide to opt out of the process. It's another way that A-Players are different.

Structured means that you ask everyone the same series of questions in the same order. That makes it easier to compare candidates.

The phone interview is your next screening and assessment tool. You will spend 45 minutes with each person and ask every candidate the same five questions. Remember to dig for specifics.

- What are your career goals?
- What are you good at professionally?
- What are you not so good at professionally?
- What are the names of your last five managers and, if I were to speak with them, how would each of them assess your performance?
- What questions do you have for me about the position?

There are plenty of people out there giving advice to job seekers. One of the standard bits is that candidates are supposed to turn a question about weaknesses into a statement of strengths.

They will tell you something like "I guess I just work too hard" or "I've been told that I push too hard for quality." Those are non-answers. You want to know the real story, and you'll probably have to push to get it. You are looking to see how honest and self-aware the candidate is about his or her strengths and weaknesses. Keep probing until you get some real answers.

Note down the questions candidates ask. Those questions will give you an idea about their career priorities and Core Values.

Wrap up the interview by thanking the candidate for his or her time and saying that you will get back to him or her about the next stage in the process. The entire phone interview process should take a maximum of 45 minutes.

Some candidates will try to force your hand by telling you that they have one or more other offers and need a response from you right away. That may or may not be true, but it doesn't matter. You need to follow your process all the way through to conclusion and make the right decision. If you miss out on this person, so be it.

There will be times when you're absolutely sure that the person you've just interviewed is the best person you could possibly hire. Don't succumb. This process will work if you work the process, but you have to work the entire process every time. Remember this great quote from Suzy Welch:

> Whenever someone appears too good to be true, the thing
> they're really good at is hiding a problem in their past.

Now it's time to select the people you want to invest some serious face time in interviewing. I usually want to interview only the top three candidates.

With three candidates, I have enough to compare. I could do more than three interviews, of course, but that takes a lot of additional time because of the length of a good interview.

Your face-to-face interviews should take three hours each. Yes, you read that right.

When I was a police officer, I learned that long interviews are the way to get to the truth. In a three-hour interview, contradictions and inconsistencies will pop out at you. You have time to return to important issues to assure that you get the truth.

In police work, there are really two different situations where you're asking questions. One is an interview. Police officers interview witnesses or victims about what happened. You ask questions that solicit all kinds of information because you don't know what may turn out to be important. When a police officer is interviewing a witness or a victim, the officer will often ask questions in ways designed to help the person remember. Officers spend time on these, but it's often spread across several sessions. Interrogations are different.

When you interrogate people suspected of committing crimes, you can assume that they will tell you whatever they think will help them look good. You have to dig for the truth. On television, that happens with brilliant questions during a short interrogation. Real life is different.

Real police officers don't do it with brilliance. They do it with persistence. Real interrogations go on for a long time, because that's what it takes to get to the truth. Topgrading interviews are like police interrogations because they're designed to identify inconsistencies and get at sometimes-uncomfortable truths. Because of that, they take a long time.

If it's a very important role, you might even have additional interviews. Those will be shorter, usually 60 to 90 minutes. Some companies, like Google, have group interviews where the candidate is evaluated by people who will be his or her co-workers.

I like tandem interviews, in which one person asks the questions while another person watches the candidate's body language and takes notes. Here's an overview of your preparation for the interview:

Review the Career History Form and notes from the phone interview to identify the things you want to learn more about. Make sure you include some questions about how they've demonstrated your Core Values in past roles and how they've demonstrated the must-have behavioral competencies that you ranked on the Role Scorecard. List the names of references you want to speak with.

Then use a structure like this example with every applicant you interview:

First, ask questions about the Career History Form to clarify any concerns you may have and/or to check that what they say matches up with what they wrote on the form:

- What exactly were you hired to do?
- What measurable results did you achieve?
- What failures or mistakes were made, and what did you learn?
- If I were to ask your immediate supervisor what your strengths / weaknesses were, what would they say?
- Why did you leave?

Second, ask behavioral competency questions specific to this role. Ask for precise examples of where they exhibited the desired behavioral competencies in their past jobs: For example, "Describe a time in your previous role when you dealt with a customer who was upset."

- What was the situation?
- Who was involved?
- What did they do?
- What exactly did YOU do? (not what "we" or "the team" did)
- What was the outcome?
- What lessons did you learn from this?

Third, ask questions to elicit examples of how they demonstrated behaviors consistent with your Core Values in the past. For example, "One of our Core Values is _____. Can you give me an example of where you demonstrated this behavior in a previous role?"

- What was the situation?
- Who was involved?
- What did they do?
- What exactly did YOU do? (not what "we" or "the team" did)
- What was the outcome?
- What lessons did you learn from this?

This is one of those situations where you have to fight what most candidates have read is the "right" way to answer a question about past performance. They think that they should appear humble and stress team accomplishments. You care about the team, but you're not going to hire the team.

You want to know what the candidate actually did and said and contributed in each situation that you ask about. You have to push and repeat and keeping peeling away the layers until you get to the truth.

Finish the interview by opening the floor to them. Ask about their career aspirations and what they expect to happen if you hire them. Try to understand what this person is really looking for in terms of a career and whether it's something you can honestly provide.

Take time to debrief with your colleague after every interview. The interviewer and the note taker should review everything. It's possible that you will want to set up another interview with the candidate, but it's not likely. If you've done a good job on the in-depth interview and taken the time, you should be ready for the next step.

You'll know which candidates are a poor fit for the role you have. Let them know they won't be going further. Thank them for their time and wish them well. Then turn your attention to the contenders who might be the A-Players you want. It's time for reference checks.

No matter how good a candidate looks, you do not offer the job until you have conducted reference checks. Everything you've done up to this point has set you up to gather the final important information through reference checks.

Specify who you want to speak with. This is usually with past supervisors and not the friends listed on the résumé. You should consider talking to past clients or customers, co-workers, and subordinates as well.

Choose the references you want to talk to and ask the candidate to set up these interviews for you. In this way, the candidate gives you his or her consent so you can get the reference's opinions. The candidate also gives the reference permission to discuss him or her with you.

This is another area where A-Players are different. They will have no problem with you speaking to past supervisors and people they've worked with. That doesn't mean everything was always rosy. There are sometimes issues in their past relationships. When that's the case, you want these issues to come out and to discuss them with the candidate before you do the reference checks. You don't want any surprises.

Just like with the other interviews, these are all done the same way, following a script. That helps you compare the results among applicants. Here's how the reference check interviews should proceed:

- In what context did you work with this person?
- Can you clarify their accountabilities and responsibilities in this position?
- What were the person's strengths?
- What were areas for improvement?
- How did you rate this individual's overall performance?
- Given the outline of the role we are recruiting for, how successful do you think the candidate will be? [Describe the Key Outcomes and Duties and KPIs for the role using the Role Scorecard]
- One of our Core Values is _____. Can you give me an example of where this person has demonstrated this behavior? [ask this for each Core Value]

Conduct the reference interviews yourself. This is not a job for HR or administrative staff. You want to hear the tone and exact words people use when describing the candidate. You want to be able to push and probe for critical points.

It's a detailed process, isn't it? It's worth the effort. Companies that use this procedure have found that it's worth doing because of the quality of the people they bring on board. Remember, if you use this entire process every time, you can raise your success rate of A-Player hiring to at least 70 percent. Many companies raise it to 90 percent. But you take shortcuts at your peril.

I know that it takes time and discipline to follow such a rigorous process. It will take you longer to hire someone. In fact, you may end up rejecting all the candidates you interview and having to start over. If that happens, so be it.

Don't be tempted to take the best of the bunch. If you are not absolutely sure you have found an A-Player, don't rationalize why you should hire a B-Player who happens to be in front of you.

Far better to start again than make a bad hiring decision and have to deal with the consequences of replacing the person down the road. Your goal is to fill every role with A-Players. It takes longer, but the results are worth it.

After you've hired A-Players, your job is just beginning. Business Execution for RESULTS requires that you provide them with the appropriate tools, training, mentoring, and support so they can do the job they're capable of. And you need to keep them motivated. That challenge begins even before the first day that your new hire shows up for work.

Onboarding and Developing People

Everybody shows up motivated for the first day on the job. Unfortunately, for many people at many companies, that's the most motivated day they'll ever have. In fact, one study by Booz and Company concluded that 15 percent of all new hires think about leaving on the very first day.

The 2012 Allied Workforce Mobility Study found that the average company loses a quarter of their new hires within a year. But you don't want to be an average company, or you wouldn't be reading this. Turning over 25% of your workforce is costly and grossly inefficient.

Note: Business Execution for RESULTS does, in fact, create an appropriate level of staff turnover. If you are holding people firmly accountable, you should be removing poor performers periodically. If you have zero staff turnover, chances are you are carrying a lot of dead wood.

If you've followed the advice in the last chapter, you're committed to using a rigorous, disciplined process to hire as many A-Players as you can. It only makes sense to help them become as productive as possible as fast as possible. That's what good onboarding processes do.

Texas Instruments compared new hires who went through an onboarding process to those who did not. They discovered that those who went through the process were fully productive two months sooner. Corning Glass determined that new hires who went through a formal onboarding process were two-thirds more likely to stay with the company for at least three years.

Onboarding

My ideas about what a good onboarding process looks like were formed by my experience in the pharmaceutical industry. The company that hired me used a disciplined process to make sure they were hiring the sort of people they wanted. The induction process was every bit as rigorous.

There was a plan that specified what I would be doing every single day for my first five weeks with the company. In the beginning, it was all product knowledge and exams. Then I learned and rehearsed the well-documented sales processes. After that, there were role-plays and making presentations in front of in-house doctors and pharmacists.

Those presentations were videoed and then critiqued while being played back on a big screen. No one continued with the process until they had mastered the presentations.

Then there was time spent in the field observing other staff doing their jobs and being introduced to customers. Finally, I was allowed to start presenting to clinicians in hospitals and medical centers, but with my manager observing and coaching me. That continued until he was completely satisfied that I could handle myself while being bombarded with questions and objections from medical professionals, and that I would represent the company's products effectively, accurately, and ethically.

I know that most companies do not have the ability to design such a thorough and detailed induction process, but the principles are the same. Your process should have two objectives: You want to create a great first impression and you want to make the new hire become productive as quickly as possible.

You may not have a full-service HR department or specialists in onboarding, but you probably have something better. If you're a small to mid-sized business, you can give a new hire personal attention, because you usually only hire one person at a time. Not only that, you're flexible and you're really excited about this new hire because he or she is going to help you achieve your BHAG.

And there's one more thing – A-Players are different. They're top performers, and they're excited about coming to work for you, because they know it's a good fit for both of you. They're going to expect you to live up to the impression you made during the rigorous hiring process.

Don't wait until their first day; reach out and ask what information they want before they start. Schedule some informal get-togethers with the people the new hires will work with. Send them notes reminding them that you know they're top performers and that you're excited about them joining the team.

Make it easy for them to do the necessary legal paperwork. You will discover that many A-Players prefer to have that all done when they show up on their first official day.

Tailor your onboarding plan to the individual and your situation. Big companies can't do that, but you probably can. Find out what the new hire wants to learn and plan to make it happen. List the things and people you want the new hire to become familiar with and help make that easy.

One small trucking company created "cheat sheets" for every new hire. The sheets listed all the people the new hire would work with regularly, along with their nicknames, a brief description of what they did, contact information, and pictures. They also created "if/then" sheets that listed routine tasks (such as submitting an expense report) with brief instructions on how to do it.

Structure the first five days on the job in detail. Make sure that the new person meets everyone he or she will be working with as soon as possible. Use lunches as a way for the new person to spend time with those people.

Remember that a new hire joining your company is probably entering a work environment that's very different from any place that he or she has worked before. The Core Values are visible, the BHAG for the company is clear, and so are the Strategic Projects and KPIs, along with single-point accountability for each one. Roles and reporting relationships are clearly spelled out on the Role Scorecard, and Role KPIs provide specific performance targets for every person.

Most people, even A-Players, are not used to the culture of relentless accountability that you will be creating with Business Execution for RESULTS. If you've followed a disciplined hiring process, you should have hired an A-Player. You should have evaluated whether your new hire has the same Core Values that you do. So that individual should fit your culture, but that can be difficult, even for the best.

Real performance and accountability cultures are rare. So there are three things you should do to help your new hire learn your cultural ropes:

Assign someone as the new hire's guide to the process and the company. The guide's job is to answer questions and help the new hire make connections during the onboarding period. Pick someone who knows the company well for this role.

Within the first day or so, you should show your new hire his or her dashboard. That's the best introduction to what his or her daily life will be like with you. Explain when and how you review performance.

Extend the onboarding period for new hires to last until the second quarterly SWOT Analysis after their hiring. That gives them the time to experience at least one full cycle from Reality Check through a quarter of performance to another Reality Check.

Keeping Your A-Players

A-Players are the people everyone wants to hire, so you can bet that other companies will approach your A-Players with employment offers. How do you keep them from jumping ship? Start by thinking about the different ways that people are "paid." Here's how it worked for me.

When I worked in the pharmaceutical industry, I received excellent cash compensation. My salary was reviewed every year, and there were all kinds of performance bonuses. They were wonderful – but salary and bonuses quickly just became "part of the package." I felt good for a couple of weeks, but they had limited effects on future performance.

In fact, when I look back on those years, I can't remember a single bonus check or what it was for. The money went into my bank account, and I used it to buy things.

Most people are like me when it comes to cash compensation. We want to make a fair income for what we do. That means fair when compared with your colleagues and with what someone in your industry should reasonably expect to receive for their responsibilities and performance. If we don't think that we're paid fairly, we get de-motivated.

Money is what psychologist Frederick Herzberg called a hygiene factor. A hygiene factor, like pay, can satisfy you, but it won't motivate you. You have to have enough to be satisfied and, if you don't, then you're dissatisfied or de-motivated.

Herzberg contrasted hygiene factors with motivation factors in his books and his classic 1968 *Harvard Business Review* article, "One More Time, How Do You Motivate Employees?" Here's how they played out in my life:

I loved the challenging work of presenting sophisticated products to arrogant, skeptical surgeons and getting past the defensive barriers they set up for themselves. I loved overcoming their objections and being perceived as an expert resource they could confide in. But what really motivated me were the training and travel experiences provided by my company.

Training is often looked at as a remedial tool for poor performers, but the type of training I was offered was a meaningful reward for me. I got sent to conferences and training courses all around the world. I would visit the head office and our many manufacturing facilities in Europe every year for in-house training. I got the opportunity to attend sales and marketing training conferences at wonderful chateaus in Europe. The medical conferences my company sponsored were often in some of the most exotic tropical island locations.

How lucky was I? I was an ambitious young man learning and growing and seeing the world. Not only that; as I moved up the corporate ladder, there were other benefits. I became sales and marketing manager for the whole of New Zealand. My company then engaged a leadership coach to work with me one-on-one for an hour every week to help me develop and become a senior leader. I felt as if the company valued me enough to invest in growing my skills. And that motivated me even more.

The specific mix of motivators I just described was unique to me. But every A-Player has a mix of motivators, and that mix almost always includes the same things.

A-Players like interesting and challenging work. They want to accomplish important things, so give them the tough, high-profile assignments. They relish handling the tough projects and making important decisions.

A-Players want to be recognized for their achievements. Make sure you praise them and use other means to tell them that you appreciate their good work.

A-Players love to learn and develop. They love courses and conferences. And no one will get more out of quality coaching than your A-Players.

If you want a company made up of A-Players, you have to design your hiring, onboarding, and daily operations to make Business Execution for

RESULTS happen. A-Players' high levels of drive and achievement orientation set them apart from other workers. But there are some ways in which all workers are the same.

All of us want to do work that engages us. That's what the next chapter is all about. When you're ready, turn the page to learn some proven ways to engage people at work.

Engaging People at Work

Engagement is one of today's hot business topics. On Amazon, there are close to 400 leadership and management books about engagement. There are thousands of magazine articles and blog posts that tell you how to create it. Every major consulting firm seems to have its own proprietary method for creating engagement. They make it too complex and mysterious.

When I was in pharmaceutical sales, I was what most people describe as "engaged." I worked hard and tried to do a little better every day. I supported the people around me.

The pharmaceutical company satisfied the hygiene factors for me. The salary and bonuses were fair compared with the rest of the industry. Working conditions were safe and clean. My colleagues were friendly and competent. Your company has to satisfy the hygiene factors, or engagement will not happen. But hygiene factors don't motivate people.

The pharmaceutical company gave me things that motivated me. There was interesting and challenging work. I had the freedom to do many things on my own. The travel opportunities were amazing. And the company gave me endless opportunities to grow and develop my skills.

Even so, I left the industry. Why? I left because I realized that I just wasn't passionate about it. I didn't get excited about improving lives by creating pharmaceutical breakthroughs. My purpose wasn't their purpose. I'm not saying it was better, just that it was different.

I didn't understand the power of purpose right away, but things came together for me when I met the people at RESULTS.com. I realized that my purpose in life is to teach people how to be more successful. They were in the business of helping companies become more successful. We were a great match. Looking back, I can see that we had a common purpose.

The broadest and most powerful engagement happens when a company has a purpose that gives people an opportunity to work for things beyond the numbers. If you're clear about your purpose, people who share the same purpose will clamor to work for you. When everyone is working "on purpose," people will give that extra measure of discretionary effort that we call engagement. Engagement helps drive Business Execution for RESULTS.

Purpose is the engine of deep, powerful engagement. To make the magic happen, though, you have to begin by defining your purpose and then sharing it with the people who work at your company.

Core Purpose

Earlier in the book I introduced you to the research that makes a solid case for increases in engagement preceding improvement in financial results. I also mentioned the research of psychologist Dr. Richard Hagberg, who found that companies with challenging goals and a clear purpose deliver the highest returns. You've worked hard to develop challenging goals. Now it's time to clarify your Core Purpose.

There are people who claim that the sole purpose of a business is making money or "maximizing shareholder value." That may be true for economists, but real people don't get excited about those things. If you want people to get excited about what they do and give effort and attention beyond the minimums, you need to give them something to work for beyond the numbers.

That something is your Core Purpose. So get your team together and work out the answers to four important questions:

Why does your company exist, beyond making a profit? Profit for a business is a lot like oxygen is for a person – you don't live to breathe, but you have to breathe to live.

What are you really passionate about? What gets you excited about what your company does?

What difference do you make in the lives of your customers? How are their lives better because of what you do?

What do you do for your customers that transcends the products or services you currently offer? What is the essence of what you do for your customers that will still be valid in ten years' time?

Work with these questions until you have a statement of the Core Purpose for your company. If you're like many companies, it will be a fairly long statement. For your Core Purpose statement to be as powerful and energizing as possible, you need to make it short and sweet.

Apply my Twitter Rule: Rephrase your Core Purpose statement in 140 characters or less. Many companies start with the word "to" or the phrase "Our purpose is to." Complete that statement so it will fit as a Tweet.

Take a look at what you've decided and what you've written down. Obviously, you think that the Core Purpose you've identified is important, meaningful, and motivating. But what about others in the company, especially those in frontline positions?

This is not easy. Many companies struggle with it. But if you can nail it, you'll find that it makes everything else better. If it were easy, everyone would be doing it. Business Execution for RESULTS is not necessarily easy, but it works.

Core Purpose is a key driver of engagement, but purpose alone won't do the trick. Remember that you must satisfy the hygiene factors. And you should add three more drivers of engagement:

People are more likely to become engaged if they do challenging work. KPIs and responsibility for projects make the work challenging for most people. The other way that work is challenging is if people are always learning more. That relates to the next engagement driver.

People want to grow, develop, and make progress. If you arrange their work so that they can do that, even a little bit every day, they are more likely to become engaged. The book *The Progress Principle* by Teresa Amabile and Steven Kramer underscores this with comprehensive research. Here's how the authors sum up their findings:

> Our research inside companies revealed that the best way to motivate people, day in and day out, is by facilitating progress – even small wins.

People want as much control as possible over their work life. They want to make choices about how to do their work. When you allow them to make those choices, they're more likely to become engaged.

There's an interesting dynamic in the way these forces work. The company as a whole is responsible for satisfying the hygiene factors such as pay, benefits, and working conditions. But an individual person's direct manager is responsible for most of the motivational factors.

On one side, bad bosses can destroy morale and productivity. A 2007 Gallup survey found that bad managers are the big reason that 56 percent of employees show up but don't put forth much effort. Gallup says that they're "sleepwalking through their days."

But good managers make a positive difference. A person's immediate boss has more impact on morale and productivity than any other single factor. That's more than "faith in top management," whether the company is a "great place to work," or anything else.

As RESULTS.com CEO Ben Ridler says, "Getting the right frontline managers in place is critical to success. When it comes to managers, I have two jobs: I'm either coaching and developing managers, or I'm looking for their replacements."

The conclusion is obvious. You want to get the best managers that you can at every level. The catch is that the only reliable guide to whether a person will be a good manager is his or her performance as a manager.

If you're hiring someone from outside, that should be one of the things you look at very closely, one of the areas where you dig deeply. You want to find out if his or her team was a top performer and also had high morale. If you're hiring for a leadership role, you want to talk to a person's peers and subordinates, as well as his or her manager. You want to hire managers judged as excellent by all three groups.

If you're growing your own leaders from within, create opportunities for the individual contributors who may want to become bosses to try on the role. Give them developmental assignments that involve leadership, such as being the project manager for one of your Strategic Projects.

Everybody wins that way: People have the opportunity to discover if the different work of being responsible for a group is something they enjoy and are likely to do well. It gives you a chance to assess them in a leadership role, too. And, as a bonus, developmental assignments are drivers of engagement because they help people grow and develop.

Use their performance when they're responsible for a group to assess whether they will be successful as managers in formal roles. Leadership writer Wally Bock suggests that you ask and answer the following questions:

- How did the person do when he or she was responsible for group performance?
- Did the team perform well given the challenges it faced? How was team morale?
- Was the person willing to make decisions? Not everyone is, and it's part of the job.
- Was the person willing to talk to others about performance or behavior? A surprising number of people shy away from this, but a good boss deals with problems when they're still small and easier to solve.
- Did the person enjoy helping others succeed? That's a characteristic of great bosses.

So now you know what to do if you want to increase the engagement among the people in your company. Alas, you won't know how well you're doing unless you find a way to measure engagement levels in your company so you can compare them over time and among units. That's harder than it seems at first.

Since there is no agreed-upon definition of engagement, there is also no commonly accepted way to measure it. To make matters worse, consulting firms large and small have tried to stake out "engagement" as their proprietary turf. They've each developed their own method of measuring engagement.

These methods are very different and vary wildly in effectiveness. In fact, Dr. Bret Simmons of the University of Nevada-Reno described one prominent firm's method as being similar to measuring the health of a tree by measuring the amount of fertilizer you applied to it.

As varied as the consulting firms' measurement schemes are, they do have one thing in common: They all require the consultants to conduct extensive and expensive surveys of your employees. At RESULTS.com, we thought that there had to be a better way.

We thought that better way should provide a reasonable assessment of employee commitment to the company. We also thought that our client firms should be able to conduct the measurement and interpret the results for themselves.

We couldn't find anything that accomplished that for engagement, but we did find something that we already used to measure customer loyalty. It's called the Net Promoter Score (NPS).

The NPS was developed by Fred Reichheld of the consulting firm Bain and Company. Reichheld focused on customer engagement, but – bear with me – methodology is relevant to our discussion on the basic principles for measuring employee engagement. NPS is based on two insights:

Satisfied customers are not necessarily loyal, and it's loyalty that you want. Think about how this works in the rest of life. You want your spouse or partner to be not just satisfied, but loyal, don't you?

You can divide customers into three groups, based on their loyalty. Some customers love your product or service. They're the ones who give you positive word-of-mouth. Reichheld called them "Promoters."

Other customers are satisfied. They like what you do just fine, but it doesn't excite them. They don't tell others about it. And if another company offered them a better deal, they just might switch. They're "passively satisfied."

A third group doesn't like you. They're difficult to deal with. They complain to you and tell others what they don't like. They're "Detractors."

Let me give you an example. Shortly before I wrote this section, the web services company GoDaddy was attacked by a hacker and shut down. Websites for hundreds of people and businesses were knocked out of service for hours.

If you were on Twitter or Facebook or any number of discussion boards that day, here's what you witnessed: There were vocal GoDaddy Detractors who used the occasion to vent their dislike of the company. There were GoDaddy Promoters speaking up for the company.

But there were also thousands of GoDaddy customers who were somewhere between those groups. They didn't offer their opinions to the public that day, but you can bet that many of them switched to other website providers soon after the incident.

Reichheld turned those two insights into an instrument to measure customer loyalty. You identify Promoters, Passives, and Detractors with a simple survey that includes one important question:

> On a scale of zero to ten, how likely are you to recommend us to someone else?

That's the basic question that determines the score. In his book, Reichheld says that you should ask that "Ultimate Question" and very little else. Questions that help you interpret answers to the ultimate question are a good choice. Here are two common ones I recommend:

> What is the most important reason for the score you gave?

> What is the most important improvement you'd like to see to make us better in the future?

The zero-to-ten scale is important because it gives you a way to quickly classify the responders. Starting with zero helps prevent the situation where responders mistake "one" for the best. And Reichheld's research has validated that customers intuitively grade your company in ways that match his definitions.

- Promoters are the people who give you a 9 or a 10 score.
- Passives give you a 7 or an 8.
- Detractors give you a 6 or below.

I found it very interesting to learn from Reichheld that someone who gives you a 7 or 8 is someone who is only satisfied, but not loyal. If you are not getting 9 or 10 scores from your customers, that means you are not good enough, and you have more work to do!

Here's the equation to calculate your Net Promoter Score:

NPS = Percentage of survey total who are Promoters, minus the percentage of survey total who are Detractors

Find the percentage of each, and you can compute a single number that measures how you're doing at building loyalty with your customers.

You can read Fred Reichheld's book, *The Ultimate Question*, for details of how he developed the measure and why it works. But you only have to look at various companies' Net Promoter Scores and their profitability to know that it works.

Take the banking industry. There, the average NPS is just 18 percent. But the financial services firm USAA has an NPS of 87 percent, according to the Satmetrix 2011 Net Promoter® Benchmark Study of US Consumers.

At RESULTS.com, we had already used the NPS model for surveying our clients. I think it's the best way for a company to get a handle on customer engagement.

We then adapted the NPS model to measure employee engagement. It may not be as sophisticated or scientific as the models used by other consulting firms, but it has two advantages – it's simple to use and it works.

It's easy to use. Just ask the people who work for you the following three questions:

On a scale of 0-10, how likely are you to recommend our company as a place to work to a friend or family member? Answers to this question give you an accurate idea of the level of employee engagement.

What is the primary reason for the score you just gave? This helps uncover important issues that need fixing.

What is the most important improvement you'd like to see to make us better in the future? This gives employees the opportunity to share the good ideas we know they have.

Administer the survey in a way that protects an individual's identity. But do it in a way that lets you segment responses by role, location, or business unit. Here are some tips for using what you learn:

- Track performance over time so you can spot changes and trends. Surveying once per quarter or once every six months seems to work well.
- One cadence that works well is to survey your customers one quarter, then survey your staff the next quarter. That way, one quarter you are looking at internal engagement and the next quarter you are looking at external engagement, but you are conducting a survey every quarter.

- Deal with specific issues that require immediate attention but avoid kneejerk, wholesale changes to your business operations based on a small number of Detractor comments.
- Look for recurring themes and clarify the root cause.
- Capture these in your SWOT analysis for the next quarter.
- Develop a solution that targets the cause and make that a Strategic Project for the quarter.

That method gives us what we are after. It's easy to create and administer. And it results in a single score that everyone can understand. Most important, it can be used to catch and deal with problems. Here's how it worked at RESULTS.com:

I've already noted that the immediate manager has the biggest impact on employee engagement. At one time, prior to our becoming a software firm, RESULTS.com had several offices delivering face-to-face consulting services to clients in the USA, Canada, and New Zealand. The Practice Manager of the office was the immediate manager for the team of consultants, salespeople, and administrative people in that office. When we spotted trouble in an individual office, usually there was a cause that involved the Practice Manager, and that's the first place we looked.

Naturally, we followed up on those things right away. When you catch problems early, they're much easier to fix. Sometimes the Practice Manager changed what he or she was doing, and the engagement scores went back up to where we like them. And sometimes we needed to change the manager to get those engagement scores to go back up.

Just about every company out there claims something like "our people are our most important asset." Unfortunately, they don't act like it. Because they don't have rigorous, disciplined processes in place, supported by Core Values and a Core Purpose, they wind up filled with people who don't quite fit and can't quite perform. Business Execution for RESULTS gives you the tools to assure that you won't become one of those companies.

You've discovered how to hire so that you select A-Players and don't settle for less. You know how to bring those top performers on board effectively and then help them grow and develop. And, in this chapter, you've learned how to engage those people, so that they meet their own needs and help your company achieve your BHAG.

There's one more thing we need to cover. In the next section, you'll learn how to keep success going. When you're ready, turn the page to the section I call "Maintaining Thrust."

Maintaining Thrust

Introduction

When I was a boy who dreamed of becoming a fighter pilot, I tried to learn everything I could about jet planes. That's when I heard about flameout for the first time.

A flameout is "the failure of a jet engine caused by the extinction of the flame in the combustion chamber." I've never seen a jet engine flame out, but I've seen a lot of flameouts in business. You probably have as well.

I've worked with several clients who started out all fired up about their BHAG, their 3 to 5 Year Strategic Moves, and their quarterly Strategic Projects. But when I checked back with them, all that energy was gone and not much had happened. They flamed out.

Just like a jet engine, those companies lost thrust. They stopped moving forward toward that BHAG, toward achieving Business Execution for RESULTS. Over the years, I've learned that there are two main reasons why companies flame out.

Some companies flame out because they lose focus. They start "chasing squirrels" and spreading their energy over many less important things than the Strategic Projects they've agreed on.

Other companies just get tired or try to take on too much, and as a result they fail to do anything well. Achieving your BHAG isn't easy, or everyone would do it. It takes hard work, and sometimes that wears people out. This kind of flameout doesn't happen all at once.

First, someone decides that "just for this week" he or she won't work on their Strategic Projects. They are too busy fighting fires and doing busywork. Then it happens again. Soon, that individual (or that company) isn't moving Strategic Projects forward at all.

There are also situations in which a person is in the red on a KPI week after week, month after month, and nobody does anything about it. That sends the message that good performance isn't important and, after a while, performance slacks off.

In this section, you'll learn how to avoid flameouts and maintain thrust. The tool we use may surprise you: meetings.

I know that meetings get a bad rap. People hate them. They think that meetings are gigantic wastes of time. In 2011, Harris Interactive surveyed more than 2,000 workers about status meetings, and 70 percent said that status meetings don't help them accomplish their work.

A Microsoft survey tracking office productivity contacted 38,000 workers around the world to identify "productivity pitfalls." Respondents reported that two out of every five days on the job were wasted. The main culprit: "ineffective meetings."

It doesn't have to be that way. In fact, if you want to become a great company, you have to hold productive meetings if you want to achieve Business Execution for RESULTS. That's what this section is all about.

In the chapter on Rolling Reality Checks and Current Priorities, you'll learn how some very successful companies use a structure of meetings to drive performance.

Two of the most important meetings in that structure are the Annual High-Level Strategic Review and the quarterly SWOT analysis, followed by setting Strategic Projects for the next quarter. You'll see a specific meeting agenda that many companies use that can help move you toward your BHAG.

Then we'll talk about operational meetings in the chapter titled "Meetings that Drive Execution." You'll learn how to make your meetings productive and interesting instead of boring time-wasters. And I'll review the three meetings we think you should have as a regular part of your working cadence.

If you're ready to turn meetings at your company from time-wasters to productivity-drivers, turn the page and we'll talk about Rolling Reality Checks and Strategic Projects.

Rolling Reality Checks and Strategic Projects

I love watching a great rowing crew in action. The boat glides through the water, propelled by oars moving in perfect rhythm. It may be the most graceful example of teamwork in the world.

In rowing, the cadence drives the crew, keeping them in sync and urging them on when they may be tired and sore. Cadence does the same thing for great companies, except that, instead of a coxswain calling cadence, they use meetings to establish the rhythm of work.

General Electric offers a good example of how this works. According to Bill Conaty and Ram Charan, "some half dozen meetings and processes spread across the year drive the GE system." These are the regular meetings for strategy review, operating plan review, and performance evaluation that drive the whole company. At ground level, there are regular monthly, weekly, and daily meetings that help keep work on track and effective.

Obviously, you won't do things exactly like GE, but you can use meetings to call cadence for your company. For a rowing crew or an army on the march, a faster cadence means that you make more progress in the same time. A disciplined meeting cadence will help you to:

- Create and update your winning strategy
- Execute your strategy faster
- Drive accountability
- Identify opportunities and remove bottlenecks faster
- Keep staff aligned and focused

Business Execution for RESULTS requires that your strategy be reviewed with the right cadence to help you analyze what has changed in your environment and decide what changes, if any, you should make. Every year, you should conduct an Annual High-Level Strategic Review to review progress, reassess your industry and take a look at your high-level strategy to make sure your 3 to 5 Year Strategic Moves still make sense.

Between Annual High-Level Strategic Reviews, you use Quarterly Strategic Review sessions to evaluate how well you're executing on your strategy and assess the impact of any changes in your operating environment – both internal and external.

The Quarterly Strategic Review and the Annual High-Level Strategic Review form the core of the cadence that drives Business Execution for RESULTS. It's also the way you make sure that you stay on course and on the way to your BHAG.

Quarterly Strategic Review Sessions

Stop me if you've heard this one: When the Apollo 11 mission went to the moon, it was off course more than 90 percent of the time.

That statement, or something very much like it, is a staple of motivational speakers, bloggers, and people who write articles about project management or strategy. It may even be true, but I can't find an authoritative source that says so. The good news is that we don't need the Apollo 11 moon mission to make the important point that you need to reassess your progress and situation frequently on the way to your BHAG and in the implementation of your 3 to 5 Year Strategic Moves.

We can look at how regular reviews worked for the BHAG of all BHAGs, the US moon mission itself. The fact is that, when President John F. Kennedy suggested the goal to the US Congress in 1961, lots of people thought he was crazy, and nobody knew exactly how it would happen.

It was a huge, difficult-to-achieve goal. Werner von Braun, the leading US space scientist of the time, said it was as hard as "hitting a bumble bee in flight with an air rifle while riding a merry-go-round."

If the USA were to land a man on the moon and return him safely to earth within a decade, it would have to blaze new paths in a number of areas. But project teams couldn't go off chasing squirrels, either. They had to keep working on smaller projects that moved the entire project forward.

That meant that everyone had to push hard almost all the time. But every team had to stop on a regular basis and assess how things were going, too. Were they moving toward their project goal? Did that goal still contribute to the greater BHAG of putting a man on the moon?

Your business has to work the same way. You need to do hard, focused work on your Strategic Projects. But you also need to stop on a regular basis to assess how you're doing. We call those Rolling Reality Checks, and the Quarterly Strategic Review sessions may be the most important.

Think of the process as a series of quarterly sprints. You work hard and race toward a finish line that's only 90 days away. It's close enough for you to see.

At the end of that sprint, the end of the quarter, you stop for a moment, put your head up, and assess how you're doing and whether anything has changed. Then you choose the Strategic Projects to work on for the next quarter and get back to work.

These sessions are critical because they help you stay focused but flexible. It's important to do them every quarter, no matter what. And it's important to do them rigorously and well. To help you do that, there's a specific agenda that's been tested by thousands of companies around the world. Here is a brief outline, followed by more detail:

- Review strategic execution from last quarter
- Redo SWOT
- Choose Strategic Projects for next quarter

The Quarterly Strategic Review can be done in as little as a half-day per quarter, if you follow this disciplined and focused agenda.

Review Strategic Execution from Last Quarter

Start by reviewing your strategic execution from last quarter. This will help you do three things:

- You'll learn how far you've come. You should be closer to your BHAG now than you were three months ago.
- You'll be able to compare actual performance with planned performance. That will help you set aggressive, but reasonable, goals for the coming quarter.
- You'll discover positive and negative lessons from the last quarter so you can bank them. Over time, the lessons will help you do better.

The first thing you should do is assess your performance for the quarter in a general way. Here are some questions you should ask and answer:

- What surprises, good or bad, happened in the last quarter?
- What were the notable achievements your team accomplished during the last quarter?
- What did you *start* doing last quarter that has been of value?
- What did you *stop* doing last quarter that has been of value?

Review Numerical Targets next. If you've followed the process I've outlined, you've set targets for 90 days, one year, and two years. These are the numbers that matter to everyone and that are tied to your forecasts and budgets. In your Quarterly Strategic Review, you're only concerned with the last 90 days. Here are some questions to ask and answer:

- What Numerical Targets did you set last quarter?
- What did you actually achieve?
- What are the reasons for the differences?

Be sure to answer that last question for both positive and negative results. I see too many companies who only analyze the shortfalls. That's important, but there's a lot of learning from your successes, too.

Now turn to those Key Performance Indicators. You've been tracking these on a weekly or monthly basis. Here are some questions to ask and answer:

- What Key Performance Indicators did you use last quarter?
- How did you perform? At what level?
- What are the reasons for poor performance or excellent performance?

How did you do on your Strategic Projects? Those big things that you wanted to get done last quarter: They're the key projects that were going to improve your company and move you forward in your chosen strategic direction.

- What were the top three Strategic Projects you chose to execute last quarter?
- To what extent did you fully execute each of those Projects?
- To what extent did each individual complete his or her individual sub-projects?

Now it's time for a little soul-searching. The following are questions about how you worked together as a team:

- How well did your team measure progress?
- How well did you keep progress visible?
- How well did your team hold each other accountable for results?

- How well did your team hold each other accountable for getting things done on time?
- What valuable lessons did you learn last quarter to make your strategic planning and execution more effective next quarter?

At this point, you should have a specific idea of how you did last quarter, what lessons you learned, and how well you worked together. Before we move on to quarterly SWOT analysis, let's revisit two of your key strategic decisions.

Review your BHAG. Is it still valid? Are you making tangible progress toward it?

Review your 3 to 5 Year Strategic Moves. Are they still valid? Are you making tangible progress toward implementing them?

SWOT Analysis

One question that many clients ask is: "Why do we have to do SWOT analysis every quarter?" The answer is simple: "Things change."

You've just completed a review of your performance during the last quarter. Today, you know more about your strengths and weaknesses than you did three months ago.

During the last 90 days, you've done things designed to change your position in the marketplace. The marketplace is different now than it was before you took those actions. Your competitors have been busy, too. What they've done has changed the marketplace.

In the Reality Check chapter, you learned that it's best to prepare your SWOT analysis in the context of your BHAG and your 3 to 5 Year Strategic Moves. They may not have changed.

But you also learned that SWOT analysis must accurately capture your current reality. The current reality is not what it was just three months ago.

So go back to your last SWOT analysis and identify what's changed during the quarter. If you need a quick review of SWOT or the details of the process, review the Reality Check chapter. Then answer the following questions for your current situation:

What are the key strengths/assets/competencies within your current business that you can leverage? List the top five in order of importance.

What are the biggest weaknesses within your current business that could be fixed or improved within the next 12 months? List the top five in order of importance. Make sure to include the issues you'd rather not discuss or that make you uncomfortable.

What opportunities can you pursue over the next 12 months (aligned to your 3 to 5 Year Strategic Moves) that will position your company for future success? List the top five in rank order.

What external threats do you need to reduce (or closely monitor) to ensure they do not derail your plans? Identify the top five and list them in rank order.

Compare the lists you just completed with the lists from last quarter. What's different today than it was three months ago? Discuss the changes and the reasons for them. When you're ready, move on to choosing your Strategic Projects for the coming quarter.

Choose Strategic Projects for the Coming Quarter

The idea of Rolling Reality Checks is simple, and it comes to a point right here. Every quarter you will take the time to review your performance from the prior quarter and bank any lessons learned. Then you'll update your SWOT analysis. Your learning and analysis of the current situation prepares you for the final step in your Quarterly Strategic Review session: choosing Strategic Projects for the coming quarter.

You can find detail on choosing Strategic Projects in the chapter titled "What Should We Do Now?" Here's a quick review of how to choose the projects that will be your Strategic Projects for the next quarter:

- Your project should address an important issue identified in your SWOT analysis.
- Your project should either improve your current business model (improve what is) or move you in the direction of your 3 to 5 Year Strategic Moves (create what will be).
- Your project should be SMART and clearly stated.

The first thing to do is identify the three top Strategic Projects that you want to address in this coming quarter. Make sure the projects you consider meet the criteria above.

Not four, not five, but three. It sounds counterintuitive, but if you focus on less, you achieve more. Some companies may choose to focus on only one Strategic Project per quarter.

Now let's sharpen your description. Strategic Projects will usually have sub-projects. Every Strategic Project or sub-project will have a due date and a single person who is accountable for completing the project on time. Define any sub-projects and their key component tasks. Make sure one person is named accountable for each item.

Before you start high-fiving and wrapping up the meeting, let's consider some ways that companies commonly set themselves up for failure instead of success. These are so common that I think they must be rooted in human nature.

Will you be able to tell when you achieve success with the Strategic Project? Your project should be stated so clearly that everyone will know when you've achieved the goal or the specified milestone and it's time to "pop the cork" and celebrate.

Are you being reasonable about what you can achieve in the next quarter? Consider this: The "business as usual" activities of your business will need to go on. Unanticipated fires will erupt and need to be fought. The amount of time that individuals will be able to work on move-ahead projects is severely limited. It's easy to overestimate.

My experience is that the most you can expect is that a person will be able to devote a half-day a week to Strategic Project work. Even at that, the urgent will drive out important project work unless people schedule the Strategic Project work before other things on their weekly schedule. That leads to another important question:

Have you overloaded anyone? Each person has a limited amount of time that he or she can devote to Strategic Project work without having other work suffer. That can happen easily if a person is assigned to work on more than one project.

Once you've made sure that you've set yourself up for success, it's time to get to work to achieve your Strategic Projects. That's what you'll work on for most of every quarter.

At the end of every quarter, you'll review your quarterly execution, redo your SWOT analysis, and choose up to three projects as Strategic Projects for the next quarter. Every Strategic Project or sub-project should have a single person accountable for achievement.

On every fourth review, once a year, you'll do something a little different. Then, you'll step back for a real big-picture look at your strategy and how it's working. We call that session the Annual High-Level Strategic Review.

The Annual High-Level Strategic Review

Many companies have an annual, offsite, strategic planning meeting. Far too often, all it entails is a look at last year's results, followed by a meaningless exercise in financial goal setting. They say something like, "Let's increase our goals by ten percent this year." And they cascade these goals down throughout the organization.

Goal setting is important. But setting goals is not a strategy. We all want to grow. But growth is not a strategy. We all want to improve our businesses. But improvement is not a strategy. We all want to be more efficient. But efficiency is not a strategy. We want to be better than our competitors. But beating our competitors is not a strategy. Neither is some version of "bigger, better, faster, cheaper!"

Strategy is understanding how your industry is likely to play out and making wise choices about the moves you need to make that will position your company for future success.

There are profound changes occurring in many industries. Business Execution for RESULTS is a discipline that requires business leaders to put down their tools once a year, get their heads out of the day-to-day business, think about those trends, and choose the right actions to address the changes. If you don't step back and look at the big picture every year, or if you do the analysis in a cursory fashion, you risk being surprised by reality.

Consider how this works using Clayton Christensen's disruption theory. As Christensen has shown for industries as diverse as disk drives and excavators, disruptive competitors often enter at the low end of the market.

This kind of potentially devastating competition won't usually be considered in routine business assessments. That's because they're in what most of the industry thinks of as the unprofitable segment of the market. Routine assessments also rarely identify threats coming from outside the industry. That's why you need a thorough Annual High-Level Strategic Review to make sure your analysis catches the first glimmer of potentially lethal competitive threats.

There's no quick and easy way to do this review. You need to go back to redo your Industry Analysis. You redo Michael Porter's Five Forces analysis.

You redo your PEST analysis. You analyze your Target Market Customers again. As Albert Einstein said, "The questions remain the same, it's the answers that keep changing." You must go back and revisit the questions and discover how the answers have changed.

Companies that have already been through the planning process described in this book should redo this industry analysis a week or two prior to their offsite meeting. That means:

- Industry Analysis
- Environmental Analysis
- Target Market Analysis

You can almost bet that your Industry Analysis will identify changes from the year before. They will usually affect the OT part of your SWOT analysis. That should start you thinking about new Opportunities and Threats. You will be considering what the changes may mean. And you'll be doing this thinking well before the day arrives for the Annual High-Level Strategic Review.

Hold the Review meeting offsite. That minimizes distractions and interruptions.

Get your team together for the offsite the night before the review to share a meal. This enables people to catch up with each other (for those who do not work in the same office), clear the air over any minor grievances so these issues don't cloud the next day's agenda, and generally talk about the business in an informal setting. Make sure you have an early night, because tomorrow will be a mentally taxing day!

Start the day like the Quarterly Strategic Review sessions; the only difference is that you use the year instead of the quarter as the time frame. We review results from the prior year and then turn the team loose to discuss the results and their implications. Ask and answer the following questions:

- What did you achieve last year?
- What did you start doing last year?
- What did you stop doing last year?
- What were your Numerical Targets, and what did you actually achieve?

- What were your Strategic Projects, and what did you actually achieve?
- What valuable lessons did you learn last year?

Now you're ready to look toward the future. Start with the vision, made up of your Core Values, your Core Purpose, and your BHAG. Companies hardly ever change anything in the vision section of the strategic plan, but it does happen. This is the opportunity for people to voice their opinions.

Industry Analysis is next. The basic analysis of what has changed and what remains the same should be done before the Annual High-Level Strategic Review Session. You and your team should discuss the implications of any changes and what impact they may have on your strategic choices. It's most productive to review each of Porter's Five Forces individually and then discuss all the changes. Remember, the Five Forces you need to analyze each year are Competitive Rivalry, New Entrants, Substitutes, Suppliers, and Customers.

Environmental Analysis considers changes that aren't caused by industry forces. You used the PEST Analysis to examine Political, Economic, Social, and Technological forces. You should already know what has changed. Discuss the implications. In recent years changes in technology have accelerated. Make sure you understand the implications of that for your business.

Let me stop here for a moment. At this point, you've done a complete Industry Analysis. So you know what's changed. Now you have to do something with what you know.

Sure, there are environmental and competitive forces beyond your control. That's just the way it is. Your challenge is to make wise strategic choices based on what you know and what you can do.

The book *Ruthless Focus* points out that we know about the predictable crises that go with growth. And the book *Stall Points* shares research that indicates that almost 90 percent of "stall points" are preventable. Your choices and strategic decisions are what make the difference.

Here's my experience: Most growth stalls occur because a strategic assumption that was once true no longer applies to your business model. The assumptions that you hold most deeply, the ones that you "know" are true and don't question, pose the greatest threat to your long-term growth and survival.

Business history should teach us that even the mightiest and most successful companies can be brought down if they ignore changes in the marketplace and the world. Consider the case of Bethlehem Steel.

Bethlehem Steel was once a symbol of industrial might. But, after more than a century of success, it went into decline and filed for bankruptcy in 2001. There are many reasons for the bankruptcy. Two of the important ones are ignoring basic changes in the marketplace and ignoring new, more productive technology.

As the steel industry changed in the 1960s and 1970s, Bethlehem kept doing business the same way. Foreign competition was changing the landscape. But Bethlehem kept doing business as it always had, ignoring the changes, even when the average price of foreign-made steel dropped below the average price for US-made steel.

The company also continued to invest in old technology, even when there was a better way. Newer competitors, like Nucor, adopted mini-mill technology to reduce both costs and competitive vulnerability. Not Bethlehem. It rode the old technology all the way to bankruptcy. The Bethlehem Steel story illustrates two common issues:

Clayton Christensen has showed how disruptive competitors often fly under the radar by starting in the low-cost, low-profit part of the industry. The only way to spot them is to take a break on a regular basis and update your Industry Analysis.

But there's another powerful force at work, too. Researcher James Utterback has documented that:

> Firms are remarkably creative in defending their entrenched technologies, which often reach unimaginable heights of elegance and design and technical performance only when their demise is clearly predictable.

That's human nature at work. When we've been successful doing things one way, we resist changing to a different way. So we invest in what we know instead of what we need. We get stuck "improving what is" when we really should be "creating what will be." The only way to beat that is to ask and answer tough questions about your situation and what you should do next.

Good, robust debate is crucial. You're probably not digging deep enough or questioning strongly enough if there aren't raised voices and an argument or two. Just remember that the purpose of this analysis and debate is to create a winning strategy that will set you up for future success in your industry.

What you decide may even cause you to change your 3 to 5 Year Strategic Moves. It will certainly affect the Strategic Projects for the next quarter.

So choose those new Strategic Projects wisely. Reset your Numerical Targets and adjust your KPIs to reflect what you've learned and decided.

Repeating this process on an annual basis is crucial to driving Business Execution for RESULTS.

Then it's time to set off on another 90-day sprint. You're more likely to make rapid progress if you maintain a rapid cadence. Meetings can help you there, too, and that's what we'll consider in the next chapter: "Meetings that Drive Execution."

Meetings That Drive Execution

The consensus expert on life in corporate America is Scott Adams's comic-strip character, Dilbert. He is the voice of all the people who contact Adams to tell him about their work and frustration. Over the years, Adams has devoted dozens of cartoons to the subject of meetings. Here's a quote from the cartoon for November 23, 2008:

> It's not a meeting until someone's time gets wasted.

Wasting time is bad enough, but some meetings also miss opportunities. Dr. Jesse Lyn Stoner helps teams improve their performance. She often observes teams at work so she can understand what issues they need to work on. That means that she attends a lot of boring meetings.

On her fiftieth birthday, she found herself in what she says was the most boring meeting of her life. Here is the way she describes it:

> I was observing a four-hour team meeting of the company's president and his eight direct reports. Sitting around a table, one at a time, each person reported what was happening in his or her area. The president asked questions. The others listened until it was their turn. There was no real discussion.

The purpose of the meeting appeared to be updating the president, but that could have been done in a number of different ways. And Stoner points out that the company missed an opportunity to tap into the collective wisdom and experience of the senior executives.

That happens more than it should. The fact is that so many people hate meetings because so many meetings are worth hating. Too many are boring and unnecessary. It doesn't have to be that way. The answer isn't to eliminate meetings; it's to make your meetings better.

Meetings can help you be more productive, not less. They can actually save you time instead of wasting it. Those constructive meetings follow the "Five Ps of Productive Meetings."

Every productive meeting has a **purpose.** Participants should know what the meeting is for. The purpose should be worth pulling people away from other productive work. It should be something that can be best accomplished by a group of people working together at the same time.

Preparation is one key to productive meetings. Every attendee should come prepared with the right data and be ready to share their perspectives in order to achieve the purpose.

Productive meetings have a clear **process,** defined by the agenda. It should describe how participants will accomplish the purpose. I think you should have a standard agenda for every recurring meeting.

Productive meetings are characterized by the **participation** of everyone present. People should be at the meeting because they have something to contribute, and participating is how they contribute.

In a productive meeting, everyone should make **progress.** They should leave the meeting better off than when they entered and have more clarity around what everyone needs to do next.

Those guidelines should hold for any meeting you call. But there are three specific meetings that you can use to drive execution and productivity. They are the Weekly Team Meeting, the Daily Team Huddle, and the One-on-One Weekly Meeting.

The Weekly Team Meeting

When Alan Mulally took over at Ford, the company was losing money at the rate of $83 million a day. He immediately changed the way his team of corporate-level executives worked together, as Professor Nancy Koehn describes:

> He eliminated all corporate-level meetings except for two he introduced: the weekly, mandatory business plan review, when the senior team reported its progress on specific goals, and the special-attention review, when executives took up issues needing in-depth consideration.

Professor Koehn described the meetings as "the highway on which Ford's leaders drove change." The weekly business plan review meetings were Ford's equivalent of what I call Weekly Team Meetings. Reviewing performance weekly keeps things on track and sets a fast but manageable cadence for the team.

In Business Execution for RESULTS, the Weekly Team meeting is all about peer accountability. Team members are accountable to each other for their performance and for supporting each other.

Before the meeting, everyone needs to prepare so they arrive ready to help make the time productive. Every person should review his or her performance, especially KPIs and Strategic Projects. Update the status in your software dashboard of everything you're accountable for. I suggest you draft a Twitter-length status update for each item to explain what is happening and what you are doing about it. Prior to the meeting, everyone should also have clearly documented the next steps, or key tasks that need to happen next to move each of their Strategic Projects and KPIs forward.

I suggest that you hold your Weekly Team Meeting at the same time every week. That helps avoid scheduling conflicts while it establishes a steady cadence for the team. You should use the same agenda at every Weekly Team Meeting.

Standardized agendas for routine meetings are powerful. They make it easier for people to prepare. Team members can build meeting preparation into their work rhythm. Here's the agenda for a regular Weekly Team Meeting that should take one to two hours:

Start on a positive note by sharing good news. Have every team member share a personal good news story and a business good news story. In addition to setting the tone, personal good news stories help team members learn about each other. Team members should use a key accomplishment from last week as their business good news story. Allow and enforce a one-minute-per-person limit, using my Twitter rule.

Review the numbers. Check the status of KPIs. Are they in the red, yellow, or green? This should be more than a simple report on results. There should be discussion and even challenges. How can you do better? What lessons can we learn? Confirm the one thing each person will do in the coming week to improve his or her numbers. Make sure this is documented as a specific task with a due date.

Review each person's projects. What's the status of each one: red, yellow, or green? Confirm the one thing each person will do in the coming week to move his or her projects forward. Make sure this is documented as a specific task with a due date.

The **Parking Lot** is the place on the agenda for items that don't fall under either KPI or Strategic Project performance review. These should be things that benefit from harnessing the collective brain power of the team.

There may be roadblocks that are preventing a person or the team from achieving their goals. There may be an elephant in the room that you all know is there but that's not being discussed, that needs to be dealt with. Or there may be a key decision that requires input and debate by the team.

Rank Parking Lot items in priority order. That way you're tackling the most important issue first. Here are a couple of other guidelines:

Set a time limit for discussing all the Parking Lot issues and hold to it, even if you only discuss one item on the list. When that happens, you don't want the other issues to either roll over to the next meeting or simply stay unresolved. Always either resolve an issue or assign a task to someone to take a specific action that will start the resolution process for items that you did not have time to discuss on the day.

This is the part of the meeting where you're most likely to have disagreement and heated discussion. That's OK if the conflict you have is productive conflict.

You should have some disagreements. If there is no disagreement, the chances are that you've got a dysfunctional team. Disagreement, even argument, is fine if people are constructively and passionately debating the issues and concentrating on those issues, while respecting each other.

We need to make it safe for people to disagree with one another. Make it safe for people to disagree with the leader as well. Your goal is to make the very best decisions in the best interests of the company.

Your Core Values are important because they guide decision making and action when there's not a clear rule. Everyone needs to know what the Core Values are and what they look like in real life. You can help that happen by making a **Core Values Story** a compulsory part of your Weekly Team Meeting. Here's how:

Everyone is required to share a story of how someone else on the team has demonstrated one of your Core Values by their actions in the previous week. It's a great way to make the Core Values clear and also praise people who've demonstrated them in their work. I suggest the following format:

"I nominate (person) for living our Core Value of (Core Value)." Then briefly describe what they did last week that demonstrated that value using my 140-character Twitter Rule.

Wrap up the Weekly Team Meeting with the **One Phrase Close**. Go around the room and have everyone share one short phrase that captures how they feel or what they're thinking at the moment.

The One Phrase Close can serve as a quick temperature check on team morale. Some people will say something motivating and upbeat. But others may say something that gives you a clue that they're not as happy as they could be. Follow up with them later to see what's up.

The Weekly Team Meeting is a powerful way to keep things on track and moving forward. But they gain strength when you do them every week. Let me warn you that you will be tempted to skip a week because there's too much work or there's a fire that needs fighting. Don't give in to that temptation. Here's the experience of a friend of mine, who owned and ran a small publishing company, in his own words:

> Part of our operating ritual was the Monday morning all-hands meeting. In about an hour and a half, we reviewed performance and what we needed to do in the coming week. My team knew that I was a fanatic about the meeting because I felt that it kept us productive and on track.
>
> When I was on an extended trip to South America, my team decided that they were just too busy to hold the regular meeting. In fact, they skipped the meeting two weeks in a row. Nobody told me that.
>
> When we held the first meeting after I got back, it was clear that things had gone off the rails. Key performance measures hadn't been met. Projects were behind.
>
> That was odd, because my team always did well when I

was gone before. It took a minute or two before one team member told me what they'd done. I turned that into a lesson for them about the importance of that weekly meeting, but it was a lesson for me, too. When you review every week, you catch problems when they're small, and it's easy to get back on track. Every week you miss, the problems get bigger, and getting back on track takes more effort.

The Daily Team Huddle

If you really want to accelerate the progress of your business, Business Execution for RESULTS requires that you don't just meet on a weekly basis; you meet every day. Obviously, you don't want a long meeting because you want to keep energy high and get people back to productive work, but you also want to assure that the work of your team is concentrated and coordinated.

That's why people in several different industries seem to have simultaneously started holding short meetings at the start of every day or every shift. The meetings go by various names including "stand-up meeting" and "morning roll call."

These daily meetings vary a lot in the issues they address and the specifics of their agendas, but they all have five important things in common: They are held at the same time and with the same agenda every workday or every shift. They are held at the beginning of the day or shift. Everyone in the work group or team is expected to attend (or call in if they can't attend in person). Everyone stands during the meeting. The meetings are very short, ten to 15 minutes at most.

Have everyone answer the following four questions – first, each person answers the first question, then they all answer the second question, and so on.

- What are you working on today?
- What is your number-one priority to get done before you leave work today?
- Any roadblocks?
- One Phrase Close: that's anything a team member wants to say.

The whole meeting should take no more than ten minutes. That's long enough to cover the important things and coordinate team effort. It's short enough to keep energy up and start the day right. It also helps you make sure all your people are focused on their most important priority and helps the team understand what is going on with other team members.

The Weekly One-on-One Meeting

At most large companies, "performance management" involves two things: There is a job description that usually includes some hiring requirements, but no performance standards. And there is an annual or semi-annual performance appraisal. There's a better way to manage performance, it's called Business Execution for RESULTS.

The Role Scorecard defines the expectations for each role, including specific performance standards and relationships. I covered this in detail in the chapter, "Hiring A-Players." The scorecards are updated quarterly to reflect changing needs and abilities.

Team leaders are the key to productivity and morale. I covered how to select and support team leaders in the chapter, "Engaging People at Work." Catch problems and challenges when they're small so it's easier to make corrections and seize opportunities.

The Business Execution for RESULTS process you've been learning in this book helps people stay on track and succeed. It helps everyone get very clear on what needs focus and on how performance will be measured.

That process includes the Weekly One-on-One Meetings. Very few companies do anything like this, but it's critical to individual and team success. It's the team leader's opportunity to review individual performance with the same discipline and rigor as team performance.

Meet with every one of your direct reports, one-on-one, every week. Choose a location where you will not be disturbed. Don't allow distractions from your phone or computer. Your meeting should take no more than a half-hour. Block out this time in your calendar and make sure you keep these appointments every week. As a manager, your number-one task is supporting your people.

Establish an agenda and time limit, and stick to them. Keep the meeting brief and focused. Here's an agenda that works:

Prepare. You and your team member should show up with the updated information you need to discuss the current reality.

Review performance. Briefly discuss each project the individual is accountable for and get a status update. Briefly discuss each Key Performance Indicator and Strategic Project the worker is responsible for and get a status update.

Agree on what will be done. Ask the person what tangible action he or she will take this week (and next) to move each goal forward or address any issues you have identified. Agree on the actions to be taken and capture these tasks in writing, including specific details and due dates.

Take away excuses. Ask what support or resources they need from you to help them succeed. As a manager, you need to provide the resources and clear the obstacles from their paths so that the most important tasks get done. You also need to keep out of their way and not overwhelm them with too many demands or conflicting priorities. Shield them from distractions to create the time and space for the most important tasks every week.

Ask if there are any other issues that they would like to raise. How are they feeling? Are there any minor grievances that are bugging them? What's going on in their lives right now? Take a sincere interest in them and their lives outside of work.

Share any issues or feelings you think are important. Performance reviews are not an annual event. Let your people know every week how they are performing, both in terms of the performance data and what you have personally observed. Let them know that you are on their side. Demonstrate your commitment to helping them succeed.

Finish on a high note. Find something they are doing well and acknowledge it. Praise is most effective if you commend the specific behaviors you want to see reinforced.

You're not done yet. The purpose of this meeting is to improve performance, so there's one more important step.

Follow up to make sure each task gets checked off as done. You get what you inspect. Holding people firmly accountable for honoring their commitments is crucial if you want to create a high-performance culture. This is not micro-managing. Give the person the freedom and autonomy to go away and determine how best to achieve each task, but follow up to close the loop and make sure it got done.

Business Execution for RESULTS doesn't happen all of a sudden at the end of a month or a quarter or a year. Ideally, you move toward your BHAG and other goals every day and every week. The meetings described in this chapter help you make sure that all your team's efforts are concentrated on important work and coordinated to get the best results. These meetings help you spot problems and opportunities early.

They're also the final piece in the system. They're the point where all that analysis and all those decisions connect with daily activity. Turn the page for a final review of what it takes to make this work.

CONCLUSION

NO ONE KNOWS AS MUCH about your business as you do.

That's just common sense, really. You're immersed in your industry, and the people who work for you are, too. They know a lot, and they've developed relationships that help them find answers that they don't know themselves. With all that knowledge and experience, why would you ask an outsider to tell you what to do? But that happens to me all the time.

When companies call me for the first time, they usually want one of two things: They may want me to tell them what to do. Or they may want me to tell them how to do what they currently do better. They are usually surprised when I tell them that I'm not going to do that.

My purpose isn't to tell you what to do. But I can help you learn to use a proven process that will let you develop the answers you need and transform them into results. This book is about that process.

In Business Execution for RESULTS, I've tried to mimic the process I've personally used at RESULTS.com in working with the leadership teams of hundreds of client firms from a multitude of industries all around the world. It uses the best of dozens of effective business practices modified to work together in a process that will help you get results.

If you've read other strategy books or used other strategy consultants, you probably found some of those modifications strange at first. For example, we at RESULTS.com start in a different place.

Jim Collins, one of the top strategy gurus, suggests that you get the right people on the bus and then figure out where to go. But how do you determine who the "right" people are if you don't know where you want to go? Different Value Disciplines require different business models and different types of people in order to make them work. Sorry, Jim, I think you are wrong: Strategy comes first.

Other consultants start with a clean sheet of paper. They begin with classic SWOT analysis for Strengths, Weaknesses, Opportunities, and Threats. When I was a young man working in the corporate world, we used to bring consultants in to help us with strategic planning and that is exactly what they did. It stopped making sense when I asked myself, how you can do that analysis without having the context of your chosen strategic direction? (Remember the example I gave you about the reactions required to be a fighter pilot?) Strategy comes first.

The companies I work with already have a business, and it's usually doing quite well. Most of them want to get to the next level. They've already got people whose talents and energy and efforts have helped the company succeed. They come to RESULTS.com because they want to succeed faster!

The first thing to do is decide which mountain to climb. Define a Big Hairy Audacious Goal, or BHAG. Then use a proven process to do the analysis, make well-thought-through strategic decisions, and then execute them to achieve that BHAG. Here's a quick overview of that process, the one I've outlined in this book.

For me, strategy means choosing the right actions to ensure your current and future success. You need to understand the forces that will likely affect your industry. Then you can make clear choices about how you are going to compete and how you will make money, both today and in the future.

Throughout the process, you need to consider both the short term and the long term. Short term is about improving the current core business and meeting the needs of today's target customers. It's about performance improvement. Long term is different; it is about forgetting the past and reshaping the business to compete more effectively in the future.

Business Execution for RESULTS poses some questions that you must ask and answer:

What is our vision for the future? What is our **BHAG** – a stretch goal to take us from being a good company to a truly great company? What are our **Core Values** – the clear rules to guide the behaviors of everyone in our firm? What is our **Core Purpose** – a real reason to get out of bed in the morning and work hard, beyond making money?

What competitive forces will impact our firm? Use Michael Porter's Five Forces analysis to understand competitors, new entrants, substitute offerings, suppliers, and customers.

What macro-forces from the world at large will affect our industry? Use the PEST analysis to examine Political, Economic, Social, and Technological forces.

What geographic areas do we plan to serve, and how will we access those locations?

Who will be our ideal target market customer? Aim for the center of the bull's-eye.

What Value Discipline will we choose? Is Operational Excellence, Product Leadership, or Customer Intimacy the best choice for us? Are we clear on what game we are playing? Are we playing to win?

Define Core and Non-Core Activities. What should we start doing and stop doing? What is our business? What should it be? What Core Activities will we perform or develop or acquire? What is NOT our business? What should it NOT be? What Non-Core Activities will we stop doing or outsource or divest?

Now you can ask and answer specific questions to guide your marketing:

- How will we **Strategically Position** our brand in the marketplace?
- What **Key Benefits** – functional, economic, and emotional – will we offer?
- What is our **Brand Promise**, the blunt, overt promise we make that will compel our target customers to take action?

That analysis will help you define your **3 to 5 Year Strategic Moves.** The question to ask and answer is: Have we clearly stated the top three moves that our company must take in the coming years to position our firm for future success in our industry?

Only now can you do **SWOT Analysis**, because now you have the context to do it well. Ask and answer the following: Based on our chosen strategic direction, what is our current reality?

Choose your **Strategic Projects.** They are the key actions to move your business in the right direction right now, during the next quarter.

Set your **Numerical Targets** by picking the right goals and milestones to aim for in the future. The right numbers are numbers that are aligned to your strategic decisions and that measure your progress toward your BHAG. You also want to choose numbers that everyone in the company understands.

Key Performance Indicators are the crucial numbers that drive success on a weekly basis. This is the ultimate, rubber-meets-the-road point where strategy connects with accountability.

Most strategy consultants stop right here. Then they either leave execution entirely up to you, or they act as if things will never change. They take their money and go home.

Business Execution for RESULTS also requires the use of software dashboards to make all your strategic decisions (listed above, in bold type) visible to everyone on your team, so that everyone in the company knows what the strategic plan is and the important things to focus on.

These software solutions provide a helicopter view of how everyone is performing, using color coding to show whether a project or KPI is on track. The software assigns tasks to specific individuals to move your strategy forward and holds people accountable to make sure those tasks are completed on time.

At RESULTS.com, we believe that you need to review your situation every 90 days. After all, your competition isn't standing still. The world changes. And your own actions have changed your situation. I don't think of execution as a long march; I imagine it as a series of sprints, separated by **Rolling Reality Checks.**

Every 90 days you should stop for a moment and review your SWOT analysis in a **Quarterly Strategic Review.** Every fourth quarter, once a year, you'll do a complete **Annual High-Level Strategic Review.** That's when you review all your key decisions to determine if they need to change.

Even that isn't enough. Business Execution for RESULTS needs to happen every day. The fact is that it's too easy to get off course, even when you're reviewing things every quarter. We use meetings to establish a success-building cadence for your business.

In the **Weekly Team Meeting**, every team reviews performance, identifies issues that need attention, and determines the most important tasks to move each project and KPI forward in the coming week and captures them in the software. Every day begins with a short, stand-up **Daily Huddle** to make sure things are on track. And every week, every supervisor has a **one-on-one meeting** with each team member to review individual performance and issues.

You may be looking at this process and thinking, "Wow, that's a lot of work!" You're right. But this is Business Execution for RESULTS.

I know that this process works because thousands of companies have gotten good results with it. It's better today than it was when I first started with the company, because it keeps changing based on new insights and on changes in the world.

The process works. But it doesn't do the work for you. You have to add the discipline to follow the process. You have to do the hard work of analysis and decision making to create a winning strategy. You have to turn that strategy into action every day.

Yes, it's hard work, but it's worth it.

Books I Would Recommend to My Younger Self

FOR MANY YEARS I READ at least one book every week. These days it seems to be an exercise in diminishing returns, with the same information being recycled and repackaged in different ways, but I am still keen to pick up every nugget of wisdom I can. More and more, I find those nuggets in business and technology blogs and articles.

Below are the books I would recommend to my younger self if I had the opportunity to go back in time. If I had been exposed to this information at the beginning of my career, I would have learned to be a better person and a better business leader sooner, and saved myself a lot of failure and heartache along the way.

I begin with some of the books that formed the foundation of my thinking on leadership, strategy, and execution. And they laid the basis for my own book, *Business Execution for RESULTS*. I owe a lot to the authors of these books. I also list books that opened my mind to different ways of thinking. The world never looked the same after I read them.

The Foundations of My Thinking on Leadership, Strategy, and Execution

The Effective Executive – Peter Drucker
I go back to this book once a year. If you only read one book on business, make this the one. I also think that anything by Drucker is worth reading.

The Five Dysfunctions of a Team – Patrick Lencioni
Builds on the work of Drucker. How to create teams that can argue productively.

First, Break All the Rules – Marcus Buckingham and Curt Coffman
Research on what the world's greatest managers actually do to manage their people.

Topgrading – Brad Smart
No more hiring mistakes.

Good to Great – Jim Collins
For me this is rehashed Drucker, but so well-known that you still have to read it.

Mastering the Rockefeller Habits – Verne Harnish
The power of regular meetings and how to use them to drive execution.

What Really Works: The 4 + 2 Formula for Sustained Business Success – William Joyce, et al
Better quality research than more well-known books from Tom Peters or Jim Collins. What successful companies really do.

Crossing the Chasm – Geoffrey Moore
The technology adoption life cycle. Why some companies make it and some don't.

The Innovator's Dilemma – Clayton Christensen
Nothing lasts forever. A great model to understand industry disruption.

Marketing Warfare – Al Ries and Jack Trout
How to win your marketing war, depending on where you currently sit in your industry.

The Purple Cow – Seth Godin
Learn how to stand out from the crowd in a meaningful way.

Permission Marketing – Seth Godin
People don't care about your advertising anymore. Learn how to cut through the noise.

Jump Start Your Business Brain – Doug Hall
A scientific approach to marketing. Take the guesswork out of your marketing messages.

Business Model Generation – Alexander Osterwalder and Yves Pigneur
A great way to visualize your key stakeholders and map out how a business makes money.

The Progress Principle – Teresa Amabile and Steven Kramer
Solid, actionable research about the power of small wins in daily work life.

Books that Opened My Mind to New Ways of Thinking

The 22 Immutable Laws of Marketing – Al Ries and Jack Trout
A marketing classic. You will see the world very differently once you read this.

Influence – Robert Cialdini
As per the song from The Who, after reading this you "won't get fooled again."

The Hero and the Outlaw – Margaret Mark and Carol Pearson
Understanding brands and archetypes at a deeper, subconscious level.

Create Your Own Life – Brian Tracy
Learn what successful people do. Apply that to your own life.

First Things First – Stephen Covey
Better than *The Seven Habits of Highly Effective People*. How to put what really matters first in your life.

How to Win Friends and Influence People – Dale Carnegie
The best book on sales ever written. Timeless. Read it once a year.

Man's Search for Meaning – Victor Frankl
Deeply moving story of survival. Those who endure have a clear reason why. What's yours?

24406746R20140

Made in the USA
Charleston, SC
23 November 2013